Warren Koontz M.D.

Dickens's Doctors

With apologies to "Phiz"

Dickens's Doctors

by

DAVID WALDRON SMITHERS

PERGAMON PRESS

OXFORD · NEW YORK · TORONTO · SYDNEY · PARIS · FRANKFURT

U.K.	Pergamon Press Ltd., Headington Hill Hall, Oxford OX3 0BW, England
U.S.A.	Pergamon Press Inc., Maxwell House, Fairview Park, Elmsford, New York 10523, U.S.A.
CANADA	Pergamon of Canada, Suite 104, 150 Consumers Road, Willowdale, Ontario M2J 1P9, Canada
AUSTRALIA	Pergamon Press (Aust.) Pty. Ltd., P.O. Box 544, Potts Point, N.S.W. 2011, Australia
FRANCE	Pergamon Press SARL, 24 rue des Ecoles, 75240 Paris, Cedex 05, France
FEDERAL REPUBLIC OF GERMANY	Pergamon Press GmbH, 6242 Kronberg-Taunus, Pferdstrasse 1, Federal Republic of Germany

First edition 1979

British Library Cataloguing in Publication Data

Dickens's doctors.
1. Physicians - Fiction
I. Smithers, *Sir*, David
823'.8   PR4553   78-40672
ISBN 0-08-023386-4

Printed in Great Britain by
Biddles Ltd, Guildford, Surrey

Contents

Acknowledgements

I am deeply indebted to a few people in the preparation of this book: to that great Dickens scholar Michael Slater for reading the typescript and making so many helpful suggestions nearly all of which I have adopted, to David Dickens for enthusiastic encouragement which cheered me on my way and to Mrs. Dawn Lambert who has typed this text again and again with dedication and without complaint.

Extracts from Dickens's works have references to their chapters so that they may be found in any edition. Other references taken from John Forster's *The Life of Charles Dickens* are given in volume and page numbers from J. M. Dent's Everyman's Library since it is easily available. Books referred to in the text appear in the bibliography at the end.

Preface

Much has been written about Dickens's concern with public health, social conditions, mental institutions, children's hospitals and the less orthodox branches of medicine. Rather less has been written about the doctors he created and much of this has been marred by inaccuracy. This book is an anthology of the medical men who live through his imagination and of some of the doctors who attended him in person. It is primarily concerned with people, Dickens's doctors, but I have added some asides especially in an introduction, an interlude and a conclusion, to provide these remarkable people with a setting but with no intention of attempting any comprehensive view of Dickens's relation to the medicine of his day. It is people who have been my main concern and no more wondrous array of medical eccentrics has ever been portrayed in fiction. Individually they vary from the dull and virtuous Allan Woodcourt, the impetuous and quick-witted Mr. Losberne and the kindly Mr. Chillip to Dr. Dundey who robbed a bank, Lewsome who supplied Jonas Chuzzlewit with the poison to kill his father, and that most amusing if often drunken scrounger Joshua Lirriper.

These medical practitioners, larger than life, some good some bad, whether in small parts or in major roles, disport themselves beyond the compass of our wildest hopes or of anyone else's most vivid imagination. They expose aspects of medical foibles, wiles, evasions, mystifications, schemes, guile and lofty lines in flattery, the modern counterparts of which are with us to this day. There is, however, one great physician most beautifully described but never named. He did not find out the nature of Mr. Merdle's complaint until after he had died, but an earlier diagnosis was hardly to be expected. Bar liked and respected him, so did Bishop and so, quite clearly, did Dickens. Physician was an attractive man, thoughtful, composed, efficient, discreet, modest and a great reader of all kinds of literature. This is a most succinct, kindly and understanding presentation of a famous doctor. However, it is the more reprehensible of Dickens's doctors who are the most entertaining. It appears that, in fiction, we take a peccant delight in false, pretentious and venal practitioners of medicine, perhaps because in life evil doctors present the imagination with such horrifying implications. Dr. Crippin and Dr. Ruxton send a shudder through us still.

One of the most complete accounts of Dickens's doctors was written over seventy years ago by Dr. John Chalmers Da Costa. He read a paper on the subject before the Philobiblon Club of Philadelphia on May 28th, 1903, and this was published in book form in 1905. It does not appear in any of our National Library Catalogues. No copy seemed to be available in this country, the Eastgate Collection at Rochester Museum did not have one nor did the Dickens Fellowship Library in London. The Philadelphia Branch of The Dickens Fellowship located a copy of the book for me in the possession of Mrs. Norah Da Costa and Dr. Luther Brady in Philadelphia copied the original paper from the records of the Philobiblon Club on my behalf.

Dr. Da Costa wrote about more than half of Dickens's doctors, he picked the best and quoted some of the finest passages about them. He appeared, however, to be put out by what he regarded as the grave reflections which Dickens had made on a great profession. He took the laxity, rascality, tortuous villany and flourishes of pomposity exhibited by some of Dickens's doctors far too seriously. He missed both the fun and the tragedy when he described Dr. Haggage as no more than "a most atrocious medical blackguard". He pined for expressions of esteem, some sign of commendation or even a little homage to medicine which would have been most un-Dickensian. He summed up by saying: "Such are Dickens's Doctors—fools, drunkards, blackguards, criminals, coarse, common, ignorant men, imposters, solemn ignoramuses, clowns, and a few gentlemen . . . . What a pity that he never delineated such a lion-heart as Abernethy's, such a lordly soul as Hunter's, such a noble career as Paget's, or such a helpful life as Gross's. The world will always be the poorer because he did not." No ! Such solemnities are not the stuff that Dickens's doctors are made of. The world is immeasurably enriched by those he did give us, blackguards and all.

There was an article on *Dickens's Doctors* by Henry Leffmann in *The Dickensian* in 1907. Dickens inspires a following all over the world, the international nature of the interest in, and enjoyment of, his work applies to his account of doctors as to everything else he wrote. So it is not surprising to find that the next article on the subject was written in Saigon by Dr. L. Schotte, Médecin de la Compagnie des Messageries Maritimes. His work *Les Médecins dans l'oeuvre de Charles Dickens* was published in 1909. He said that the doctors in Dickens had only been given minor roles, none with a place comparable to that of Sarah Gamp, and commented that it was easy to see the reason: "La pruderie anglaise est proverbiale, la lecture est un délassement de famille, et rien, dans le roman qui passera entre toutes les mains ne doit choquer qui que ce soit." Dickens's novels seen as family entertainment which had to exclude doctors from prominence because they were too shocking to susceptible English readers to be allowed major roles is, at least, an unusual interpretation of the great man's purpose.

In England, Dr. W. H. Maidlow wrote *A Note on Charles Dickens and The Doctors* in 1917 which referred to the philosopher, Dr. Jedler, as though he were medical and included Dr. Kutankumagen amongst the people to be found in *American Notes*. He was followed in the same journal in 1922 by Dr. T. H. G. Shore on *The Doctors of Dickens* who repeated the Dr. Jedler error, saying that he had "retired from practice", failed to include Ben Allen amongst the medical students who qualified and remarked on the curious fact that Dickens included no apothecaries in his works: one apothecary in *Nicholas Nickleby* has a speaking part although his only words are "Cheer up, sir!", while another fails to mix the prussic acid strong enough for Mr. Mantalini when he poisons himself for the seventh time. A calm apothecary looks after Paul Dombey at School and a parish apothecary's assistant leaves the bedside of Old Sally in *Oliver Twist* to allow Mrs. Corney to be alone with her when she dies. Dr. Shore also referred to Sir Tumley Snuffim as the only titled practitioner (Sir Parker Peps, with his high class practice and love of titles would have had something to say about that).

Frank Green included a chapter on The Medical Profession in his book *As Dickens Saw Them* published in 1933. In 1935, back in America again, Dr. H. Pomeranz of New York wrote on *Dickens's Doctors*. His special interest was in those doctors who had attended Dickens professionally and in their famous contemporaries. He did, however, make a number of references to doctors created by Dickens. This is an interesting and generally accurate account although Dr. Pomeranz does say that the legal gentlemen in the works of Dickens outnumber the medical men. About the same time Dr. T. B. Layton in England was writing a lovely piece on *Dickens's Medical Students*. Robert Neely followed his book *The Lawyers of Dickens and Their Clerks* with *Doctors, Nurses and Dickens* in 1939, an excellent account with a good illustration of Sir Parker Peps by Donna Neely who sadly failed, however, with Betsy Prig and Sairey Gamp. Dr. Edward Raymond Easton wrote on *Doctors in Dickens* in *The Dickensian* in 1945. In 1951 Bernard Darwin chose the subject of Dickens's doctors for his Lloyd Roberts Memorial Lecture. This lecture was reported in *The British Medical Journal* but, unfortunately, was not published in the *Proceedings of the Royal Society of Medicine*. This was a delightful occasion for not only was the lecture given by the outstanding essayist of his generation, with a deep love of, and long acquaintance with, the works of Dickens and a special affection for Bob Sawyer, but the chair was taken by Sir Francis Walshe, the then President of the Royal Society of Medicine and one of the great medical writers and raconteurs of his day.

In 1970, the centenary of Dickens's death, there was naturally a spate of Dickensiana and, not to be outdone, the medical profession produced for example, *Dickensian Doctors* by Kathleen Irvine which appeared in *Pulse, Dickens and The Doctors* by James Doggart in *The Practitioner*, and *The Longer I*

Live the More I Doubt the Doctors by Robert Bathel in *St. Mary's Hospital Gazette.*

Forty-nine medical men appear by name in the works of Dickens if we count Physician as indeed we must, fifty if we include Dr. Ginery Dunkle, Dr. Dundey, and Mr. Peartree as perhaps we shouldn't, but quite a few more creep in anonymously. The lawyers (of whom there are nearly half as many) are handled, on the whole, more roughly and less sympathetically—Jaggers always excepted, along perhaps with such characters as Mr. Wickfield, dear Traddles and Mortimer Lightwood. The muster of physicians and surgeons is supported (if supported is the right word) by a horrifying if captivating set of nurses. The largest assemblage of medical talent occurs in the early works with a superficial collection of purveyors of amusing nonsense in *Sketches by Boz* and *The Mudfog and Other Sketches,* the fabulous group of doctors and medical students in *Pickwick Papers* and that bewitching, if wholly lamentable, batch of doctors and nurses in *Martin Chuzzlewit.* No medical practitioner is named in *Barnaby Rudge, The Old Curiosity Shop, Hard Times, Great Expectations* or *Our Mutual Friend* but some medical reference is to be found in every one of the novels.

The doctors, as they follow one another in each of these books (dated here by the year of their publication) closely reflect the development of Dickens's art, as that inspired story teller, unrivalled creator of fabulous characters, ardent reformer and brilliant novelist mellowed and added gravity and craftsmanship to his exuberant creativity. G. K. Chesterton wrote of his work that "Real primary creation (such as the sun or the birth of a child) calls forth not criticism, not appreciation, but a kind of incoherent gratitude."

Introduction

Dickens was born in the reign of George III, was a reporter aged 18 when George IV died and had his first book published in the reign of William IV just before Queen Victoria came to the throne; he died during Gladstone's first term as Prime Minister when Victoria had reigned but 33 of her 64 years.

Jenner had given his account of vaccination against smallpox 14 years before Dickens was born, and Laennec, the great clinician who invented the stethoscope, died when Dickens was 14. Claude Bernard the founder of clinical science was almost his exact contemporary, William Osler was born when he was 37, Simpson introduced chloroform and Warren and Bigelow used ether for anaesthesia while Dickens was writing *Dombey and Son*. Semmelweiss, who tackled "child-bed fever" so effectively by cleanliness, was born and died within Dickens's life-time having been treated with contempt by his colleagues while Lister's antiseptic system and Pasteur's germ theory of disease, which confirmed Semmelweiss's work and provided the reason for his success, were not announced until 8 years after Dickens was dead. Koch's discovery of the tubercle bacillus came 17 years after Dickens had died and Röntgen was not to discover x-rays for another 8 years after that.

Medical practice, and the hierarchy of medical practitioners were different in Dickens's day from those which we are now used to; they were, however, busily acquiring a new temper. We can appreciate this change rather better in the work of some of Dickens's contemporaries. In Anthony Trollope's *Doctor Thorne*, for example, published in 1858 between *Little Dorrit* and *A Tale of Two Cities*, there are eight medical practitioners of very different standing in the community, some of whom are old friends from *Barchester Towers*. There is the hero, Dr. Thorne, a sound, sensible, conservative practitioner, his arch enemy Dr. Fillgrave backed by Mr. Rarechild and Dr. Century, the great man from London Sir Omicron Pie, the travelling Dr. Easyman whose health, in a curious reverse relationship, is guarded by his wealthy employer Miss Dunstable, Gregson the London apothecary and Mr. Bolus who makes one brief appearance. Dr. Thorne is a graduated physician "entitled beyond all dispute to call himself a doctor according to all the laws of all the colleges". Although trusted and loved by his patients he is despised by Dr. Fillgrave as a pseudo-doctor, half-apothecary, both for the small fees he charges and because he may be seen "deeply engaged in some derogatory branch of an apothecary's mechanical trade" in the shop "not even in the seclusion of his study far from profane eyes". On the rare occasions when they meet by chance Dr. Fillgrave and Dr. Thorne bow to each other with cold propriety.

Those who prepared and sold drugs were first known as apothecaries (from the Greek for a place to store things); chemist derives from alchemist and pharmacist (the title preferred today) from the Greek for a drug. Since no one title adequately covers that elaborate medical hierarchy of early-Victorian times, I have at times in this book used the term "doctor" rather loosely to apply to any medical man, as we still do today, with the sanction of the *Shorter Oxford Dictionary* ("*pop.* any medical practitioner"), when so referring to those who have not acquired a University degree of M.D.

A year after Dickens died, George Eliot in *Middlemarch* was to provide, in Mr. Lydgate, a fine example of professional and social advance by the new men in medicine and of the usual hostility they provoked in the old, this time by their ideas rather than by their dispensing, and by their manner rather than by the fees they charged. Lydgate eventually became a success financially, alternating his practice between London and a Continental bathing-place, but he had failed as a man and as a research worker through weakness of character and a passive, selfish, socially ambitious wife with a far stronger will. He would also have failed with the research project which George Eliot selected

Dr. John Elliotson, 1786-1868.
By permission of the Royal College of Physicians of London.

Dr. James Wilson, 1795-1882.
From a print in the library of the Royal College of Physicians of London.

Dr. John Conolly, 1794-1866.
From a print in the library of the Royal College of Physicians of London.

Dr. Ernest Hart, 1836-1898.
From *Contemporary Medical Men*, John Leyland Provincial
Medical Journal.

Dr. Thomas Southwood-Smith, 1788-1861.
From a print in the library of the Royal College of Physicians of London.

Mr. Thomas Wakley, 1795-1862.
From a print in the library of the Royal College of Physicians of London.

Dr. Andrew Jackson Howe, 1825-1892.
From *Daniel Drake and His Followers*. O. Juettner, Cincinnati, 1909.

for him, since Raspails' research for the "fundamental tissue" which he followed came to naught, but neither Dr. Lydgate nor George Eliot could know that.

One of the great explosive periods of medical advance was to occur during the years immediately after Dickens's death. Unsupported assertion as the main mode of argument and uncritical peristence with a combination of bleeding, purging, vomiting and mostly useless potions as the mainstay of treatment, were yielding to a willingness by doctors to acquire a more scientific outlook, and to show greater concern over testing the quality of their remedies. That outstanding trio of physicians at Guy's Hospital, Richard Bright, Thomas Addison and Thomas Hodgkin, illustrious representatives of the new medicine, were all Dickens's contemporaries. When *Pickwick Papers* was published as a collation in 1837, Bright was 48, Addison 44 and Hodgkin 39. Bob Sawyer ought to have been a pupil of three of the most famous physicians ever to be on the staff of a London teaching hospital at the same time, but he must surely have been at Guy's well before their day—Dickens's doctors are mostly creatures of his past even though some of their most painful lineaments have not yet entirely vanished from the practice of medicine.

Dickens's doctor friends tended towards the unorthodox. Some of them favoured those fringe branches of medicine amongst which small elements of imaginative advance have yet to overcome natural resistance and to be extricated from the vast amount of illusion, myth and downright nonsense in which they are so often embedded. There was certainly much in the orthodox medicine of his day to excite scepticism and engender ridicule; however, many doctors shared Dickens's distrust of current remedies and were sympathetic to his enquiring mind and reforming zeal. Dickens was free enough with his criticism of doctors and not above an occasional sally into the field of therapeutics on his own account. On the departure from Genoa of an English physician he wrote a comment, in a letter to his biographer John Forster, which might have been made by his father in the style which was to become Micawber's:

We are very sorry to lose the benefit of his advice — or, as my father would say, to be deprived, to a certain extent, of the concomitant advantages, whatever they may be, resulting from his medical skill, such as it is, and his professional attendance, in so far as it may be so considered. (Forster, 1.103.)

Other letters to Forster written on holiday by the sea illustrate Dickens's reactions to medical emergencies and their treatment. From Brighton in 1849, where he had taken lodgings with John Leech, the artist, and his wife, both his landlord and his landlord's daughter went raving mad and the lodgers had to be driven away to the Bedford Hotel.

If you could have heard the cursing and crying of the two; could have seen the physician and nurse quoited out into the passage by the madman at the hazard of their lives; could have seen Leech and me flying to the doctor's rescue; could have seen our wives pulling us back; could have seen the M.D. faint with fear; could have seen three other M.D.'s come to his aid; with an atmosphere of Mrs. Gamps, straight-waistcoats, struggling friends and servants, surrounding the whole; you would have said it was quite worthy of me, and quite in keeping with my usual proceedings. (Forster, 1.47.)

Later in the year at Bonchurch he developed a cough which he treated, characteristically, by mounting daily to the top of the downs; when it did not disappear he became depressed and was convinced that the place did not suit his constitution, naturally making no allowance either for infection or for the creative difficulties and growing excitability he was experiencing over the writing of *David Copperfield*. He expressed the opinion that:

The longer I live, the more I doubt the doctors. I am perfectly convinced, that, for people suffering from a wasting disease, this Undercliff is madness altogether. The doctors, with the old miserable folly of looking at one bit of a subject, take the patient's lungs and the Undercliff's air, and settle solemnly that they are fit for each other. (Forster, 1.54.)

One of Dickens's medical friends was Dr. John Elliotson, for a time professor of medicine at University College Hospital, who used mesmerism in treatment. He was forced to resign his chair when he made the mistake of employing, as mediums, Elizabeth and Jane O'Key who were exposed as frauds. Anaesthesia was about to displace the use of mesmerism in surgery but Elliotson had success with hypnosis for many minor operations. He was a well known, good and enquiring physician if rather credulous; he introduced Laennec's stethoscope to Britain at St. Thomas's Hospital. Dickens and another artist friend, George Cruikshank, attended one of the operations he performed under hypnosis. Thackeray dedicated *Pendennis* to John Elliotson, and felt that he had been badly treated; it is said that he used him as a model for Dr. Goodenough. Dickens tried mesmerism himself both on his wife in America n 1842 and, with some success, on another occasion. This was when he was on holiday with John Leech who had a serious accident while bathing. Leech was knocked over by a great wave and received a severe blow on the forehead. First he was treated by having "twenty of his namesakes on his temples" but got worse; he was in excessive pain so the doctors put ice to his head continuously and bled him. For some reason he still did not improve:

> Leech has been seriously worse, and again very heavily bled. The night before last he was in such an alarming state of restlessness, which nothing could relieve, that I proposed to Mrs. Leech to try magnetism. Accordingly in the middle of the night I fell to; and, after a very fatiguing bout of it, put him to sleep for an hour and thirty-five minutes. A change came on in the sleep, and he is decidedly better. I talked to the astounded little Mrs. Leech across him, when he was asleep, as if he had been a truss of hay . . . . What do you think of my setting up in the magnetic line with a large brass plate? 'Terms, twenty-five guineas per nap'. (Forster, 1.55.)

In 1851 Dickens took his wife who had been ill to Malvern, on the advice of Dr. Southwood Smith, for treatment by Dr. James Wilson. While she was there they suffered terrible blows through the death of Dickens's father and of their baby Dora Annie within two weeks of each other. Later that year, however, he wrote, jointly with Mark Lemon, a farce, *Mr. Nightingale's Diary*, about a hypochondriac who arrives in Malvern with his daughter Rosina to take the cure, in which he acted six of the roles when it was performed at Devonshire House.

For a time Dickens became interested in phrenology and in the "water-cure". In *American Notes* when changing coaches the passengers are shown into a miserable room with a mighty jug of cold water on the table to which refreshment they so apply themselves "that they would seem to be, one and all, keen patients of Dr. Sangrado". His friend Edward Bulwer-Lytton wrote a book, called *Confessions of a Water Patient*, but George Cruikshank had a better judgement when in the frontispiece of *The Comic Almanac* he drew illustrations of the popular cold water cure in six fantastic scenes, one of which shows an attendant using a watering can on a man in bed and saying "Ah! Ah! you see wat de foolish beebles calls de dampa sheets! is very nice healsey things." However, in those days of gross overeating, fresh air and cold water for bathing and drinking may have been better remedies than those so often supplied by doctors.

In many of Dickens's novels there are passages which demonstrate a remarkable ability for clinical observation. His description of Smike's "hectic fever" was reprinted verbatim in two of the leading medical textbooks of his day (Aitken's *Science and Practice of Medicine* and Miller's *Principles of Surgery*). Two examples provide some indication of the quality of sympathetic medical insight to be found in his work. The first is taken from *Trial for Murder* in *Doctor Marigold* (named Doctor by his Cheap Jack father after the doctor who attended his birth on a common "in consequence of his being a very kind gentleman and accepting no fee but a tea-tray"). In this tale the foreman of the jury, haunted by the ghost of the murdered man bent on seeing himself avenged, describes his symptoms:

I was not ill, but I was not well. My reader is to make the most that can be reasonably made of my feeling jaded, having a depressing sense upon me of a monotonous life, and being "slightly dyspeptic". I am assured by my renowned doctor that my real state of health at that time justifies no stronger description, and I quote his own from his written answer to my request for it.

How perfectly that describes the feelings we experience when anticipating trouble or fearing some particularly unpleasing reaction, feelings which become so unnecessarily exaggerated in the early hours of the morning. Renowned doctors are still pronouncing on "real" states of health in patients suffering from anxiety or weighed down by conflict and responsibility. Not all of their patients are, of course, being harried by a determined ghost. The second comes from *Hard Times* (2, Ch. 9) at the death of Mrs. Gradgrind who is described as:

A little, thin, white, pink-eyed bundle of shawls, of surpassing feebleness, mental and bodily; who was always taking physic without any effect, and who, whenever she showed a symptom of coming to life, was invariably stunned by some weighty piece of fact tumbling on her; . . . Mrs. Gradgrind, weakly smiling, and giving no other sign of vitality, looked (as she always did) like an indifferently executed transparency of a small female figure, without enough light behind it.

She is a querulous invalid, a martyr to the symptoms which protect her from her husband with his square wall of a forehead, wide, thin and hard set mouth and inflexible, dry and dictatorial voice. As she dies she speaks with her daughter:

"Not at all well Louisa. Very faint and giddy".
"Are you in pain, dear Mother?"
"I think there's a pain somewhere in the room," said Mrs. Gradgrind, "but I couldn't positively say that I have got it".

Her protective symptoms were always most precisely localised, her vaguely wandering terminal pain is described with miraculous insight.

Dickens's best known clinical descriptions are those of the effects of head injury, minute and accurate accounts which must surely have been derived from his own observation. His picture, for example, of Mrs. Gargery's concussion, disturbance of vision, impairment of hearing and memory, auditory aphasia, cortical word-deafness and personality change following a blow over the posterior part of the brain was presented well ahead of the relevant experimental work on cerebral localisation. Eugene Wrayburn's condition, described a few days after the murderous attack on him by Bradley Headstone, is equally perceptive.

Cerebro-vascular accidents are also well described. Mrs. Skewton after a stroke recovers the use of her right hand before she can speak and then confuses names and develops a tremor before her last stroke. Sir Leicester Dedlock's stroke is brought on by the shock of Mr. Bucket's revelations about his wife's past.

Miss Havisham found her way into medical eponomic nomenclature when Dr. Macdonald Critchley wrote of "The Miss Havisham Syndrome" that may follow catastrophic disappointment, bereavement or rejection, usually in domineering, intelligent, aristocratic beauties. They hold back time, exclude the day and, dressed in the costume and jewels of their prime, seclude themselves in rooms preserved intact and filled with past associations. Macdonald Critchley quoted the Florentine beauty Virginia Comtesse de Castiglione and Oscar Wilde's mother Jane Francesca Elgee as two examples. Interestingly he proposed Queen Victoria as one of the sufferers from "The Miss Havisham Syndrome" who eventually recovered, interesting in that Dickens was writing *Great Expectations* at the very time that the Prince Consort died.

Dickens gives us some fascinating psychiatric studies such as the senile dementia of Old Chuffey and of Mrs. Smallweed, the schizophrenia of Mr. F's aunt ("An amazing little old woman, with a face like a staring wooden doll too cheap for expression, and a stiff yellow wig"), the hysterical paralysis of Mrs. Clennam and of Tommy Traddle's mother-in-law, Mrs. Crewler, ("whatever occurs to harass her usually settles in her legs"), and the chronic hypomania of the man over the garden wall who so intrigued Mrs. Nickleby. There are many other medical descriptions such as the bronchitis and emphysema of the lobster-eyed, blue-faced, panting, wheezing Major Bagstock, the rosacea of Mr. Mould's assistant undertaker, the pituitary dysfunction of the Fat Boy in *Pickwick Papers,* Flintwich's torticollis and Newman Noggs's unilateral exophthalmos. There are also the mentally subnormal such as Barnaby Rudge, Mr. Dick, Maggy after an illness at the age of 10, and Sloppy. Dickens was led astray into defending his account of the spontaneous combustion of Krook and again in his venture into a form of telegony. The latter was when the birthmark on the wrist of Barnaby Rudge was attributed to his mother having clutched the wrist of his murderous father in terror a few days before he was born but, as Edgar Allan Poe pointed out, it should at least have been the murderer who clutched his wife's wrist.

The doctor in *The Old Curiosity Shop* (Ch. 46) who sees Little Nell, after she is first taken ill and rescued by the old schoolmaster, is a red-nosed gentleman with a great bunch of seals dangling below a waistcoat of ribbed black satin. He takes stock of the situation, feels her pulse, looks at her tongue and eyes the half-emptied wineglass of brandy and water as if in profound abstraction.

> "I should give her—" said the doctor at length, "a teaspoonful, every now and then, of hot brandy and water".
> "Why, that's exactly what we've done, sir!" said the delighted landlady.
> "I should also", observed the doctor, who had passed the foot-bath on the stairs, "I should also", said the doctor, in the voice of an oracle, "put her feet in hot water, and wrap them up in flannel. I should likewise," said the doctor with increased solemnity, "give her something light for supper—the wing of a roasted fowl now—"
> "Why, goodness gracious me, sir, it's cooking at the kitchen fire this instant!" cried the landlady. And so indeed

it was, for the schoolmaster had ordered it to be put on, and it was getting on so well that the doctor might have smelt it if he had tried; perhaps he did.

"You may then", said the doctor, rising gravely, "give her a glass of hot mulled port wine, if she likes wine—"

"And a toast, sir?" suggested the landlady.

"Ay," said the doctor, in the tone of a man who makes a dignified concession. "And a toast - of bread. But be very particular to make it of bread, if you please, ma'am".

With which parting injunction, slowly and portentously delivered, the doctor departed, leaving the whole house in admiration of that wisdom which tallied so closely with their own. Everybody said he was a very shrewd doctor indeed, and knew perfectly what people's constitutions were; which there appears some reason to suppose he did.

Another of Dickens's medical comments occurs in *Barnaby Rudge* (Ch. The Last) when John Willet has a stroke:

> Being promptly blooded, however, by a skilful surgeon, he rallied; and although the doctors all agreed, on his being attacked with symptoms of apoplexy six months afterwards, that he ought to die, and took it very ill that he did not, he remained alive—possibly on account of his constitutional slowness—for nearly seven years more, when he was one morning found speechless in his bed.

Another of Dickens's medical friends was Dr. John Conolly who wrote a book on "non-restraint" in asylums, an innovation by which suitable patients, previously shackled and chained, were freed to move about the hospital. He was noted for the reform he introduced into Hanwell Asylum. He was so unjustly used by Charles Reade, who made him the model for Dr. Wycherley in *Hard Cash*, first published in serial form by Dickens in his periodical *All The Year Round*, that it called forth the wrath of the profession. Dickens was forced to deny responsibility for the views of his contributors. In another of his para-medical activities Dickens also worked with Dr. Ernest Hart, the secretary of the

Association for the Improvement of the London Workhouse Infirmaries of which Dickens was a member.

Dickens had dealings with that surprisingly versatile man, Dr. Thomas Southwood Smith, a Unitarian Minister who also practised medicine in Yeovil but came to London in 1820. He was concerned with sanitary reform and did much to influence Dickens's campaign for better housing and the abolition of the terrible sanitary conditions in slum dwellings. Jeremy Bentham left his body to Southwood Smith to be dissected and preserved and Dr. Smith duly dissected and lectured over it in 1832. He kept the skeleton dressed in Bentham's clothes in his Finsbury Square consulting room. It is now with his many manuscripts in University College, London.

In *The Uncommercial Traveller* (Dullborough Town, Ch. 12) Dickens revisits by train (engine no. 97 S.E.R.) his boyhood home which he had left in a stage-coach. The station had swallowed up the playing fields and beyond it was a tunnel. This was surely Chatham, situated between two tunnels, but the S.E.R. locomotive no. 97 was an 0-6-0 goods engine unlikely to have hauled a passenger train except in an emergency.

> I had not gone fifty paces along the street when I was suddenly brought up by the sight of a man who got out of a little phaeton at the doctor's door, and went into the doctor's house. Immediately, the air was filled with the scent of trodden grass, and the perspective of years opened, and at the end of it was a little likeness of this man keeping a wicket, and I said, "God bless my soul! Joe Specks!"

He follows him in and in the waiting-room he finds a portrait of Mr. Specks, bust of Mr. Specks, silver cup from grateful patient to Mr. Specks, presentation sermon from local clergyman, dedication poem from local poet, dinner-card from local nobleman and a tract on balance of power from local refugee, inscribed *Homage de l'auteur à Specks*. Joe has married Lucy Green and is a busy and respected general practitioner.

There are some other doctors in *The Uncommercial Traveller*. On jury service Dickens had to help decide whether a servant-of-all-work had committed a minor offence by concealing a birth or the major offence of killing her child. He paid a tribute to the humanity and good sense of Mr. Wakley, surgeon and coroner, and commented on the doctor who gave evidence that he "was a timid, muddle-headed doctor, and got confused and contradictory, and wouldn't say this, and couldn't answer for that . . ." as other doctors, before and since, have sometimes behaved when confronted with the majesty of the law. In *The Great Tasmania's Cargo* there is a horrifying description of the state of the soldiers landed from the ship and taken to the Liverpool workhouse suffering from starvation, dysentery and scurvy. The medical officer stoutly confronts the official Pangloss (repeatedly maintaining that everything done and provided was the best possible) with the terrible evidence of disgraceful neglect, appalling conditions, and callous treatment.

A Small Star in the East contains a description of the "East London Children's Hospital", an old sail loft or storehouse bought and fitted up by a doctor and his wife. The goods are hoisted up and down through two trap doors in the floor. There are 37 beds and a devoted group of nurses who help them run this remarkable enterprise. One comment represents an attitude not unknown to full-time doctors in a National Health Service when confronted with foreign patients:

> When this hospital was first opened, . . . the people could not possibly conceive but that somebody paid for the services rendered there; and were disposed to claim them as a right, and to find fault if out of temper.

British citizens, who having paid for them, are able to claim medical services as a right, are remarkably seldom "out of temper", indeed most are over appreciative and far too tolerant of delays.

In *American Notes* Dickens wrote a moving account of conditions in the Eastern Penitentiary of Philadelphia. It was here that he saw the terrible effects of solitary confinement. Locked in behind double doors, through a trap in which food was passed, he watched men seated at work, one at a loom and another at his trade of shoemaking, one of whom had been there, completely alone for eleven years. He was told that on first being confined the prisoners were stunned and abandoned themselves to despair but that when they did rouse themselves from a stupor they cried through the trap in the door "Give me some work to do, or I shall go raving mad!" Dickens was to write of Miss Havisham that her mind, brooding solitary, had grown diseased, as all minds do and must and will that reverse the appointed order of their Maker. This horrifying experience in Philadelphia was later to be turned to good effect by Dickens in his account of the imprisonment of Dr. Manette.

In Boston, Dickens met Dr. Howe who had achieved a miraculous feat of education with Laura Bridgman, an intelligent child who was blind and deaf, had no sense of smell and little taste. In contrast, in Bellville, a small collection of wooden houses huddled together in the very heart of the bush and swamp, he met Doctor Crocus (Ch. 13) who lectured on Phrenology:

> "Walk in, gentlemen, walk in! Don't be ill, gentlemen, when you may be well in no time. Doctor Crocus is here, gentlemen, the celebrated Dr. Crocus! Doctor Crocus has come all this way to cure you, gentlemen. If you haven't heard of Dr. Crocus, it's your fault, gentlemen, who live a little way out of the world here: not Dr. Crocus's. Walk in, gentlemen, walk in!"

Dickens may have been too easily misled by ill founded ideas in medicine for, astute though he was, he had had no scientific training in the skills of refutation, but being an expert in the study of human nature he was not the man to be taken in by charlatans.

When Dickens died in 1870 *The British Medical Journal* spoke for the Medical Profession when it said "What a gain it would have been to physic if one so keen to observe and so facile to describe had devoted his powers to the medical art." *The Lancet* on the same occasion said "Medical science, particularly in its bearings on the community as distinct from the individual, requires organisation — the establishment and maintenance of centres of relief, such as dispensaries, hospitals and convalescence homes. Depending as they do on voluntary support, they flourish or languish in sympathy with the liberality or the selfishness of the public. To soften this selfishness, to quicken this liberality, was the task to which Charles Dickens devoted himself—not after the mode of a licensed inculcator, but in obedience to the love of mankind with which his warm heart and genial imagination glowed."

Illustrations of Dickens's Doctors

Slammer of the 97th was the first of Dickens's doctors to be illustrated and the only one to be drawn by Robert Seymour. In the autumn of 1835 Seymour had the idea of publishing a series of humorous sketches of sporting life connected by individuals who would be members of a cockney club and were to have ludicrous adventures due to want of skill and grotesque incompetence. He prepared some sketches and showed them to the publishers, Chapman and Hall, who undertook their presentation, paying him a fee for each etching. Someone was needed to supply a more or less coherent narrative to link these sketches together. A number of people were approached, one of whom, Charles Whitehead, was recorded in the *Dictionary of National Biography* as having recommended his friend Charles Dickens for the job so becoming his most important literary benefactor; this may be a myth sponsored by Whitehead himself who was apt to suppress evidence of his own indebtedness to Dickens. At the time Dickens was a parliamentary reporter but he had just written some sketches under the name of "Boz", illustrated by George Cruikshank who drew that temporary medical student Septimus Hicks and illustrated *Oliver Twist* including a picture of Mr. Losberne. Mrs. Seymour was consulted by her husband and declared that *Sketches by Boz* "created no amusement in her" but suggested, nevertheless, that Dickens be allowed to write the text as "fifteen pounds a month, poor fellow, will be a little fortune to him".

Dickens, unknown and only 23 years of age, proved difficult to direct, he was no sportsman, produced highly successful ideas of his own and was soon directing the artist. Things moved fast: the first terrible number appeared on April 1st, 1836, Dickens was married on April 2nd and Robert Seymour committed suicide on April 20th. Seymour was suffering from depression but must have suffered quite a lot from Dickens too. Although landed with Seymour's original scheme Dickens seized the opportunity provided by the scope of a long serial and was soon changing the plan to suit his own talents and inclinations. He set off along his assured path of destiny towards his certain fame despite the conjugal bias of Mrs. Seymour who said that he would have been "consigned to obscurity for the remainder of his days, unless Mr. Seymour had permitted him to edit the Pickwick Papers". It is hardly surprising that *Pickwick Papers* started badly, it was episodic and hastily improvised; never intended to be a novel it was nevertheless developed by Dickens into a lop-sided masterpiece displaying both an invention and execution far beyond anything he had achieved in *Sketches by Boz*.

The first picture containing a doctor was later entitled "Doctor Slammer's Defiance of Jingle". From the start Dickens was imposing his will for he had the position of Dr. Slammer's right arm altered in Seymour's, original sketch. The drawing which eventually appeared in Chapter 2 was done by Hablôt Browne ("Phiz") and was almost an exact copy of Seymour's, though Jingle was considerably improved. Before "Phiz" took over the illustrations, there had been an unfortunate trial of Robert Buss, two of whose pictures were issued with Part 3 ("the suppressed plates"). Robert Buss was a painter of consequence, doing portraits and subject pictures. He had had some success as a painter of humorous incidents but this was not his real line and he was entirely ignorant of the practice of etching. However, he put aside a painting he was doing for the Royal Academy and attempted to produce in a hurry the pictures urgently needed for the next number of *Pickwick Papers*. He put his drawings in the hands of an engraver who sent the plates straight to the printer. The result was a disaster. Robert Buss said they were "designs of which not one touch of mine was on the plates". His association with *Pickwick Papers* came to an abrupt end. However, he was not lost to Dickensiana since the fine unfinished painting he started later on, entitled "Dickens's Dream", has become the most widely known of all the Dickens portraits. In it the author is depicted sitting in his chair, drawn back from his desk (now with the picture in the Dickens Fellowship Museum in Doughty Street) with visions of many of his characters in miniature floating around the room before him.

So "Phiz" was brought in and took over the task of illustrating the first editions of Dickens's works for the next 23 years. He added incalculably to the appeal and to the appreciation of so many of Dickens's characters but also greatly enhanced the situations and the settings in which many of them moved. Some of our most lasting impressions of Dickens's work are revealed, particularly in crowd scenes, through drawings made by "Phiz", such, for example, as the activities of the two mobs below the balcony at the Eatanswill election or all those boys at Dotheboys Hall seen thrice, the second time watching Nicholas astonishing the whole assembly by beating Mr. Squeers with his own instrument of torture.

So "Phiz" drew all the originally published pictures of Dickens's doctors until Marcus Stone took over for *Our Mutual Friend*. As well as the copy he made of Seymour's drawing of Dr. Slammer, "Phiz" drew Bob Sawyer, Ben Allen, Lumbey, Jobling, Bayham Badger, Harold Skimpole, Physician and Alexander Manette. His illustrations are the perfect complement to Dickens's text, meeting the author's rigorous demands and combining a delicacy of line, a brilliance of invention, and an extension of humour which greatly intensify the whole effect. The pictures he drew have never been replaced in our minds, his people are Dickens's people, his Sam Weller is our Sam Weller, in a way in which none of the many able illustrators who followed have ever quite achieved—close to it though "Kyd" (J. Clayton Clarke) was to come with his pictures of individual characters.

When Hablôt Browne died in 1882 *Punch* paid the following tribute to him:

> The lamp is out that lighted up the text
> of Dickens, Lever—heroes of the pen.

> *Pickwick* and *Lorrequer* we love, but next
>   We place the man who made us see such men.
> What should we know of *Martin Chuzzlewit*,
>   Stern *Mr. Dombey*, or *Uriah Heep?* —
> *Tom Burke of Ours?* — Around our hearts they sit,
>   Out living their creators — all asleep!
> No sweeter gift e'er fell to man than his
>   Who gave us troops of friends — delightful "PHIZ".

The illustrations for *Our Mutual Friend* were drawn by Marcus Stone. His father Frank Stone was a friend of Dickens. Marcus had drawn some pictures for six of the books when they appeared in cheap editions before his work for *Our Mutual Friend*. He had made one drawing of Dr. Alexander Manette in ragged clothes sitting on a stool looking none too frail. His work lacked "Phizs' " quality of fantasy, he added no dimension of his own, his creatures were good solid people.

I incline to the view that in *Our Mutual Friend* Marcus Stone only drew one doctor, though he may have drawn two. When Rogue Riderhood is run down in his wherry by a foreign steamer and brought into the Six Jolly Fellowship Porters likely to die, he is hurried to a first floor bedroom by the capable Miss Abbey Potterson. He makes a remarkable recovery, acquiring the belief that he will never die from drowning. The illustration shows him beside the bed dressing himself having refused to stay there as ordered. The drawing shows a little crowd of spectators round the door but only five people are in the room: Rogue himself putting on his coat, Pleasant, his daughter, and three bewhiskered men. The text leads us to expect a larger gathering: Tom Tootle, Bob Glamour, William Williams, Jonathan of no surname, and the doctor as well as the Riderhoods. Which two can have left before the moment depicted? Those remaining are described as "the ring in which he has had that little turn up with death". One of those who left must surely be the doctor for not only do the three who are still there all look like seafaring men but many a patient has got out of bed and started to dress the moment his doctor left the room.

The case for a doctor being seen at Eugene Wrayburn's bedside is a far better one. Mortimer Lightwood is on one side and Lizzie is on the other while Jennie Wren sits by a table at the end of the bed. The shadowy, and appropriately grave, figure seen behind Lizzie must surely be the medical attendant. Mr. Milvey came in later but if this had been he then Bella Wilfer should have been in the room as well. So Marcus Stone must have done one of the original drawings of a Dickens doctor, though this one remained unnamed.

Marcus Stone has a special claim to the regard of Dickens devotees in that he told Dickens about Willis a taxidermist who lived in Seven Dials and it was on him that Mr. Venus was modelled. Dickens visited Willis's shop but never met him; the background was enough to inspire the creation of the fabulous taxidermist and osteologist who bought Silas Wegg's right leg (the side had been decided by Marcus Stone, Ch. 7).

"Where am I?" asks Mr. Wegg.

"You're somewhere in the back shop across the yard sir; and speaking quite candidly, I wish I'd never bought you of the Hospital Porter".

"Now, look here, what did you give for me?"

"Well", replies Venus, blowing his tea: . . . "I'm not prepared, at a moment's notice, to tell you, Mr. Wegg".

"Come! According to your own account, I'm not worth much", Wegg reasons persuasively.

"Not for miscellaneous working in, I grant you, Mr. Wegg; but you might turn out valuable yet, as a" — here Mr. Venus takes a gulp of tea, so hot that it makes him choke, and sets his weak eyes watering: "as a Monstrosity, if you'll excuse me."

Original Illustrations of Dickens's Doctors

1	The Boarding House (Hicks)	Cruikshank
2	Dr. Slammer's Defiance of Jingle (Slammer)	Seymour and Phiz
3	Mr. Pickwick Slides (Sawyer and Allen)	Phiz
4	The Drinking Party at Bob Sawyer's (Sawyer and Allen)	"
5	Mr. Bob Sawyer's Mode of Travelling (Sawyer)	"
6	Oliver waited on by the Bow Street Runners (Losberne)	Cruikshank
7	Emotion of Mr. Kenwigs on Hearing the Family News from Nicholas (Lumbey)	Phiz
8	The Board (Jobling)	"
9	Coavinses (Skimpole)	"
10	The Family Portraits at Mrs. Bayham Badger's (Badger)	"
11	Sir Leister Dedlock (Skimpole)	"
12	The Patriotic Conference (Physician)	"
13	Under the Plane Tree (Manette)	"
14	Vignette Title (Manette)	"
15	The Shoemaker (Manette)	"

Sketches by Boz (1836)

The first of Dickens's doctors appears in *The Four Sisters* and is instrumental in solving a mystery in a small inquisitive community, namely which one of the Miss Willises Mr. Robinson has really married. They had all been seen to leave the house together and to travel with him to church and they all appeared to join in the responses. *The Four Sisters* has no illustration but George Cruikshank did a sketch for one which was not used showing all the four Miss Willises swooning at the altar rail. When Mr. Robinson went to live in their house after the ceremony the neighbours were still left in a terrible state of suspense speculating about which of the four had succeeded in the capture. Mr. Dawson "the surgeon etc." clinches the matter when he attends Mrs. Robinson's confinement and the youngest Miss Willis becomes a mother.

Dr. Wosky, Mrs. Bloss's physician in *The Boarding House* is adept at turning public credulity to good effect; he has plenty of money acquired by invariably humouring the worst fancies of all the females he is introduced to.

> "We must take stimulants, plenty of nourishment, and, above all, we must keep our nerves quiet; we positively must not give way to our sensibilities. We must take all we can get", concluded the doctor, as he pocketed his fee, "and we must keep quiet."
>
> "Dear man!" exclaimed Mrs. Bloss, as the doctor stepped into his carriage.

The first part of The Boarding House introduces a temporary medical student, Mr. Septimus Hicks: "a most interesting person; a poetical walker of the hospitals, and a 'very talented young

22

man' ", who only reads Byron and quotes from *Don Juan*. As soon
as he has married Matilda Maplesone he leaves both medicine
and marriage behind: "having walked the hospitals took it into
his head to walk off altogether". A house-surgeon gives evidence
on the nature of injuries received by a woman in *The Hospital Patient*. A young medical practitioner in *The Black Veil* at last sees
his first patient, to whom he is taken by the man's mother, only to
find that he has just been hanged. The parish doctor is cursed in
a tale of unmitigated gloom and horror called *The Drunkard's
Death*. Thank heaven that Pickwick was to come!

The Mudfog and Other Sketches, Bentley's Miscellany (1837)

No less than twelve doctors are named as attending the *Anatomy and Medical Section Meetings of the Mudfog Association for the Advancement of Everything,* that irreverently mocking disparagement of those solemn, over earnest and quite unproductive communications which are made at times to the Annual Meeting of the British Association for the Advancement of Science (founded in 1831), and not to that august body alone. There is much to be said for the occasional application of a little facetious ridicule to the behaviour of important people attending the meetings of great institutions, it can have a most salutary effect in dispelling complacency and diminishing pomposity. It does, however, become a bit tedious if it isn't mollified by insight and founded on a basis of real understanding. In these early sketches Dickens came too close to ill informed scoffing for them to be accepted as more than amusing burlesque.

At the meeting Dr. Kutankumagen (of Moscow) reports a case in his own practice:

> . . . strikingly illustrative of the power of medicine, as exemplified in his successful treatment of a virulent disorder. He had been called to visit the patient on the 1st April, 1837. He was than labouring under symptoms peculiarly alarming to any medical man. His frame was stout and muscular, his step firm and elastic, his cheeks plump and red, his voice loud, his appetite good, his pulse full and round. He was in the constant habit of eating three meals *per diem,* and of drinking at least one bottle of wine, and one glass of spirituous liquors diluted with water, in the

24

course of the four-and-twenty hours. He laughed constantly, and in so hearty a manner that it was terrible to hear him. By dint of powerful medicine, low diet, and bleeding, the symptoms in the course of three days perceptibly decreased. A rigid perseverance in the same course of treatment for only a week, accompanied with small doses of water-gruel, weak broth, and barley water, led to their entire disappearance. In the course of a month he was sufficiently recovered to be carried down-stairs by two nurses, and to enjoy an airing in a close carriage, supported by soft pillows.

Iatrogenic disease (that caused by doctors) has been on the increase since Dickens's day, for doctors now have a wider scope for the exercise of their belief in cures; they have invented a whole ingenious range of most imaginative remedies to replace mere bleeding, only a small proportion of which are genuinely curative. The vast improvement in public health since the time Dickens wrote about has been due more to changes in our environment, to such things as better sanitation, improved nutrition, adequate housing, cleanliness and more suitable clothing than to anything directly attributable to curative medicine. The abolition of places like Tom-all-Alone's, on which Dickens himself had so great an influence, has had a far greater impact on public health than any amount of pills and potions. Remarkable progress has been made, however, in many fields of medicine, notably in reparative surgery, in the control of infections and deficiency diseases, and in prevention which has, for example, in 178 years, virtually banished from the world the terrible scourge of smallpox which Jo gave to Esther Summerson and which so marred her beauty. Most doctors, nevertheless, deal with individuals rather than practice environmental or community medicine, people are their right concern; as soon as they put other things first the essential spirit and the required dedication depart and the practice of medicine declines.

At the Mudfog Association meeting a curious case was also reported of the medical student who was tried and executed for committing a burglary to a large amount under unusual circumstances. He attended the *post-mortem* examination of a man who had inadvertently swallowed a door-key which had left such a true representation on his stomach mucosa that the student was able to take an impression of it. He made a duplicate key, entered the man's house and robbed it, leaving us to wonder (amongst other things) how a key which had been swallowed "in early life" was still the one used to open the man's front door.

Mr. Pipkin (M.R.C.S.) relating the sad tale of a homoeopathist, Sir William Courtenay (they were knighting them then), said:

> The section would bear in mind that one of the Homoeopathic doctrines was, that infinitesimal doses of any medicine which would occasion the disease under which the patient laboured, supposing him to be in a healthy state, would cure it.
>
> Unfortunately Sir William was shot, and no-one present possessed the power of reasoning by analogy, or carrying out a principle. Had he been treated with an infinitesimal dose of lead and gunpowder immediately after he fell he would have recovered forthwith. But the unfortunate Gentleman was sacrificed to the ignorance of the peasantry.

Some of the Mudfog doctors have remained. We have our anecdotal addicts with their love of irrelevant detail, so apt in literary fun and so dreary and unprofitable in case reporting. The best case reports are those used to refute a theory: one swallow may not make a summer but the sight of one black swan does knock the universal white-swan-hypothesis for six. We also have with us a growing band of deeply scientific doctors who wouldn't dream of stooping to anecdotal medicine but whose presentations of the most complicated experimental work, though packed with statistical analyses, adorned with charts and laced with diagrams, fail to relate their findings to an clearly stated hypothesis which they are seeking to refute. We are in danger of becoming submerged in data, swamped with facts, buried in beliefs and deprived of reason. There is scope for a more mature, up-to-date and better informed parody of the proceedings of some of our modern Mudfog Associations.

Pickwick Papers (1837)

The Pickwick doctors are a glorious collection. There are those military surgeons: Slammer of the 97th, who challenged Mr. Winkle to a duel and Payne of the 43rd and that eminent Barts' surgeon Slasher ("Best alive") whose skill was so great (Ch. 32) that it was said of him that he:

> Took a boy's leg out of the socket last week — boy ate five apples and a gingerbread cake — exactly two minutes after it was all over, boy said he wouldn't lie there to be made game of, and he'd tell his mother if they didn't begin.

Slasher had no call for acupuncture.

From time to time depressing and extraneous stories break into the irregular flow of this hilarious narrative with its astute and jovial display of character — the converse of those comic interludes introduced between the acts of long morality plays. I never liked them and used to skip them as a boy. "A Madman's Manuscript" read at a late hour by Mr. Pickwick in the village of Cobham when he was unable to sleep is particularly distressing. The mad-man has full knowledge of his fearful family history and of his own, so far undetected, state of mind. He despises the needy relatives of the girl he marries who, loving another, is sacrificed by them to gain a little of his wealth. Following an abortive attempt which he makes to cut her throat with a razor, she faints and, after being bereft of animation for hours, regains consciousness raving wildly and furiously. The passage which follows (Ch. 11) is a description of an alarmingly possible nightmare consultation:

> Doctors were called in — great men who rolled up to my door in easy carriages, with fine horses and gaudy servants.

They were at her bedside for weeks. They had a great meeting, and consulted together in low and solemn voices in another room. One, the cleverest and most celebrated among them, took me aside, and bidding me prepare for the worst, told me—me, the madman!—that my wife was mad. He stood close beside me at an open window, his eyes looking in my face, and his hand laid upon my arm. With one effort, I could have hurled him into the street beneath. It would have been rare sport to have done it; but my secret was at stake and I let him go.

The main Pickwick group of doctors are introduced on Christmas Day and we follow two of them from medical school to foreign practice. They revolve around Bob Sawyer, one of my favourites among the many Dickens's doctors—heartily approved of by Sam Weller, which is a firm mark in his favour. Bob and his fellows: Benjamin Allen, Jack Hopkins, Noddy, Gunter, a pale youth with a plated watch-guard and a prim personage in clean linen and cloth boots form an unforgettable band. They are so up-to-date in their talk, clothes and manners that they could (almost) be at Guy's or Bart's today, though not, of course, at Thomas's or George's. They let drop little gems of conversation (Ch. 30) for Mr. Pickwick's benefit:

"Nothing like dissecting to give one an appetite."
"I've put my name down for an arm, at our place."

and of someone fallen out of a four pair of stairs' window and not expected to live

"Rather a good accident brought into the casualty ward."
"There must be a splendid operation though, tomorrow—magnificent sight if Slasher does it."

Their clothes are the gear of today. Gunter wears a shirt emblazoned with pink anchors (Jermyn St.), Jack Hopkins (a Bart's man) a black velvet waistcoat, thunder-and-lightning buttons, a blue striped shirt and a white false collar (Carnaby St.) and Bob Sawyer (of Guy's) a coarse blue coat, a pair of plaid trousers and a large rough double-breasted waistcoat (Kings Road, Chelsea). Bob's manners, like his clothes, are ahead of his time for he effects a slovenly smartness and a swaggering gait, smokes in the streets and calls waiters by their Christian names.

Ben Allen, Bob's constant companion from school to Bengal, isn't really in the same class: he is coarse, stout, thick-set and embellished with spectacles, presenting a mildewy appearance, with black hair cut rather short and:

> although there was quite enough of his face to admit of the encroachment of a shirt collar, it was not graced by the smallest approach to that appendage.

Ben's sister Arabella, by making off with Mr. Winkle, thwarts his plan to make Bob master of her one thousand pounds. Mr. Robert Sawyer, the realist with a good heart, knows better:

> "She's a very charming and delightful creature, and has only one fault that I know of, Ben. It happens, unfortunately, that that single blemish is a want of taste. She don't like me."

When Bob goes into practice in Bristol he adopts a far more original method of advertising than Mr. Dawson, Mrs. Robinson's (née Willis) *accoucheur* who had merely displayed a large lamp outside his house with a different colour in every pane of glass. Bob, however, gets his boy Tom to leave medicine marked "From Sawyer's, late Nockemorf's. Physicians" at the wrong houses (Ch. 38) so that he may call to collect them next day:

> "Very sorry—his mistake—immense business—great many parcels to deliver—Mr. Sawyer's compliments—late Nockemorf."

One four-ounce bottle, which wasn't done yet, had been to half the houses in Britsol. To add to the impression thus created his boy rushes into church with horror and dismay depicted on his countenance to fetch Bob out just before the psalms, that strategic moment when people have nothing to do but look about them:

"Bless my soul", everybody says, "somebody taken suddenly ill ! Sawyer, late Nockemorf, sent for. What a business that young man has !

A better idea than having your name flashed on the screen at a Royal Society of Medicine meeting with only doctors to impress.

Despite all his efforts Bob is forced to the conclusion that his chances of deriving a competent independence from the honorable profession to which he has devoted himself is rather dubious. He makes a precipitous departure from Bristol by suddenly boarding Mr. Pickwick's carriage, leaving the business to take care of itself as it seems to have made up its mind not to take care of him. To Sam Weller's delight he jerks his leathern knapsack into the dickey, jumps on the roof of the chaise, gives a prolonged imitation of a key-bugle, changes hats with Sam, ties a crimson flat to the rail, produces an enormous sandwich and a goodly-sized case-bottle and proceeds to exchange lively badinage with any passing stranger. This situation, with Mr. Pickwick, in alarm, leaning out of the chaise window is depicted in one of "Phiz's" fine illustrations.

One of those tidy endings imposed on Dickens by the demands of his readers as they followed every move in the fortnightly parts, produced a sorry end to Bob's career. Surely he was wasted on the East India Company in Bengal where this grand doctor after contracting yellow fever fourteen times was forced into abstinence, a sad fate for one who had prescribed so soundly for Mr. Pickwick when he fell through the ice into the pond, saying that there was nothing like hot punch in such cases, and that if hot punch ever did fail to act as a preventative it was because the patient had fallen into the vulgar error of not taking enough of it.

Oliver Twist (1838)

The parish surgeon who ushers Oliver into his world of sorrow and trouble does such matters by contract and on this occasion is assisted by a pauper old woman referred to as Mrs. Thingummy or Old Sally who has been rendered rather misty by an unwonted allowance of beer. Not misty enough, however, to prevent her from robbing the dead mother of a pawn ticket found to represent a small kid bag containing the evidence of Oliver's identity. It is a matter of some doubt whether the child will survive to bear any name at all since there is considerable difficulty in inducing him "to take upon himself the office of respiration". However, being in a workhouse he survives. Had he been surrounded (Ch. 1) during this brief period while he struggled for breath by:

> careful grandmothers, anxious aunts, experienced nurses, and doctors of profound wisdom, he would most inevitably and indubitably have been killed in no time.

The memoirs of Oliver Twist might then have possessed:

> the inestimable merit of being the most concise and faithful specimen of biography, extant in the literature of any age or country.

Miserable, starved, beaten, degraded, saved from a chimney sweep only to be sold to an undertaker and then trained as a pickpocket, at last he makes his first escape. At Mr. Brownlow's, recovering from his fever (Ch. 12), Oliver finds a gentleman by his bed with a very large and loud-ticking gold watch in his hand who feels his pulse:

> "You *are* a great deal better, are you not, my dear?" said the gentleman.

"Yes, thank you sir", replied Oliver.

"Yes, I know you are", said the gentleman. "You're hungry too, an't you?"

"No, sir", answered Oliver.

"Hem!" said the gentleman. "No, I know you're not. He is not hungry, Mrs. Bedwin", said the gentleman: looking very wise.

The old lady made a respectful inclination of the head, which seemed to say that she thought the doctor was a very clever man. The doctor appeared much of the same opinion himself.

"You feel sleepy, don't you, my dear?" said the doctor.

"No, sir", replied Oliver.

"No", said the doctor, with a very shrewd and satisfied look. "You're not sleepy. Nor thirsty. Are you?"

"Yes, sir, rather thirsty", answered Oliver.

"Just as I expected, Mrs. Bedwin", said the doctor. "It's very natural that he should be thirsty. You may give him a little tea, ma'am, and some dry toast without any butter. Don't keep him too warm, ma'am; but be careful that you don't let him be too cold; will you have the goodness?"

The old lady dropped a curtsey. The doctor, after tasting the cool stuff, and expressing a qualified approval of it, hurried away: his boots creeking in a very important and wealthy manner as he went down stairs.

Mr. Grimwig comes to tea with Mr. Brownlow, having first ascertained that there are muffins in the house (Ch. 14), and expresses his suspicion of boys, surgeons and orange-peel:

There's always more or less orange-peel on the pavement in our street; and I *know* it's put there by the surgeon's boy at the corner. A young woman stumbled over a bit last night, and fell against my garden-railings; directly she got up I saw her look towards his infernal red lamp with the pantomime-light. "Don't go to him", I called out of the window, "he's an assassin! A man-trap!" So he is.

Re-captured by Fagin, Oliver is used by Bill Sikes in a burglary and is shot by Mr. Giles. It is then, over half-way through the book that the only named doctor to appear in *Oliver Twist* comes into his life. Mr. Losberne, surgeon and doctor to Mrs. Maylie and Rose "bursts into the room" at his first appearance, and from then on is deeply committed to everything that occurs. He is one of Dickens's good doctors: a jovial, teasing, energetic, gentle, kind, hearty, eccentric, old batchelor who is described on five separate occasions as being impetuous. He has grown fat, more from good-humour than from good living, never acted on anything but impulse all his life and has the warmest respect and esteem of all who know him.

Mr. Losberne arrives to find Oliver in Mrs. Maylie's house having been shot in the arm after climbing through the scullery window and being abandoned all night in a ditch by Bill Sikes. He is impressed by Oliver's story and is entreated to save the boy by Mrs. Maylie's adopted niece Rose Fleming. He takes charge at once: Oliver's wounded arm is soon "bound and splintered up", a story prepared, witnesses confused, evidence fabricated and the Bow Street officers fobbed of with a highly doubtful story and a series of strange coincidences to the effect that an innocent lad, accidentally wounded by a spring-gun in a boyish trespass has happened to call at the house for assistance on the very morning after an intruder of the same age has been shot while forcing an entry. A useful type of G.P. to have by you in an emergency!

Mr. Losberne represents a development in Dickens's treatment of medicine. The earlier doctors have been bizarre caricatures presented as an amusing but distinctly sardonic burlesque. Mr. Losberne is the first doctor to be treated at all seriously as a doctor, and he is treated well. He is a man known through a circuit of ten miles round as "the doctor". He welcomes being called out to visit his patients (unlike a few doctors today), indeed he remonstrates with Mrs. Maylie for not sending for him at once in an emergency, arrives late at night from Chertsey to the cottage "at some distance in the country" when Rose is taken ill and sees her through the crisis of her fever. The worthy doctor returns to Chertsey when it is all over: Fagin, Sikes and Nancy dead, Monks gone abroad to squander his inheritance and die in prison, Rose and Harry Maylie married and Oliver adopted by Mr. Brownlow with his name established and his three thousand pounds secured. But Mr. Losberne is restless after all his adventures, so he settles his practice on an assistant, takes a cottage near a village, contracts a strong friendship with Mr. Grimwig and takes up "gardening, planting, fishing, carpentering and various other pursuits of a similar kind": all undertaken with his characteristic impetuosity. In each and all, he becomes "famous throughout the neighbourhood, as a most profound authority".

Oliver Twist is an immensely popular work, it caught the public imagination and has been made into films, presented on television and staged both as a play and as a musical. It competes with *Barnaby Rudge* for the title of Dickens's first planned novel. *Barnaby Rudge* was projected as a serious historical novel, under the title of *Gabriel Vardon the Locksmith of London*, but was shelved for five years when the phenomenal success of *Pickwick Papers* changed Dickens's life and set the bearing of his work. Instead *Oliver Twist* was started while he was still working on the eleventh number of *Pickwick*. Banking on his sudden great success he was careful not to move too far from the style which had just brought him fame, while breaking away from the form which had been imposed on him by *Pickwick* without losing the advantage or the challenge which a serial presentation offered. At this time, he was not only writing two books simultaneously but he was editing a monthly magazine and Grimaldi's autobiography as well; he was also enlarging his friendships and extending the social life which was so necessary to his self expression. When *Barnaby Rudge* eventually appeared, *Pickwick Papers*, *Oliver Twist*, *Nicholas Nickleby* and *The Old Curiosity Shop* were behind him and, though still concerned with the Gordon Riots and the burning of Newgate prison, it was certainly a very different book from the one he had originally planned. In *Oliver Twist* the extraordinary genius of the man shines through the intense pressure of work but the result still shows signs of immaturity, the characters are either too good and too dull to have sufficient substance, like Oliver himself, or so bad and so very much alive as to absorb the

Plate 1. The Boarding House (Hicks).

Plate 2. Dr. Slammer's Defiance of Jingle (Slammer).

Plate 3. **Mr. Pickwick Slides (Sawyer and Allen).**

Plate 4. The Drinking Party at Bob Sawyer's (Sawyer and Allen).

Plate 5. Mr. Bob Sawyer's Mode of Travelling (Sawyer).

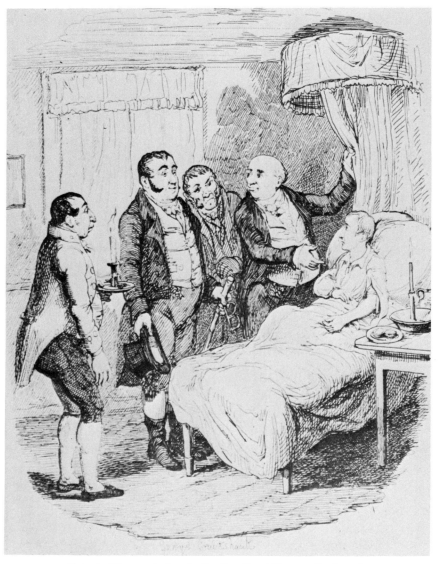

Plate 6. Oliver waited on by the Bow Street Runners (Losberne).

Plate 7. Emotion of Mr. Kenwigs on Hearing the Family News from
Nicholas (Lumbey).

Plate 8. The Board (Jobling).

whole interest. We delight in the glorious gang of villains, revel in Fagin, Sikes, Nancy and the Artful Dodger, find exciting drama in the death of Nancy and the hounding down of Bill Sikes without being much moved or responding, as we are surely meant to do, by condemning the evils in society which lie at the root of crime. It is fun, but lacks both the depth and the effective reforming influence his later work was to achieve.

Nicholas Nickleby (1839)

There are those who consider that, as a novel, *Nicholas Nickleby* fails. Oh, to have written such a failure! No doubt it is not a perfectly constructed melodrama, it is, however, packed with glory, crammed with joy, overflowing with characters and might almost be counted as a masterpiece on the presentation of Mrs. Nickleby and Mr. Crummles alone, and a vast step forward in Dickens's development as one of the greatest of all creators of fictional characters. This is the point at which Dickens comes alive as a really great artist and not only as a brilliant characaturist and story teller.

There are few doctors in *Nicholas Nickleby* and those who do appear play little part in the drama. However, they provide wonderful embellishments to the scene when they are discovered. Anonymous, and probably imaginary, doctors are credited with having ordered Sir Mulberry Hawk abroad after the story of his sorry showing against Nicholas' challenge has got about; his cowardice and injury are "noised in all directions" until "every club and gaming-room rung with it". Twice anonymous doctors predict an imminent death for Smike, the first of them providing Brooker with the opportunity of having him presumed dead while he packs him off to Dotheboys Hall, but the second giving a more accurate prognosis at the time when Nicholas takes him off to Devonshire with "rapid consumption". Two doctors only appear by name, Sir Tumley Snuffim and Doctor Lumbey, with practices located at rather different levels in the social scale.

When the name of Mantalini appears in the list of bankrupts, Kate Nickleby has to seek employment outside the millinery and dressmaking business and goes as companion to Mrs. Wititterly. The Wititterlys live in Cadogan Place, that connecting link "be-

tween the aristocratic pavements of Belgrave Square and the bar-
barism of Chelsea". On this doubtful ground Mrs. Wititterly
spends most of her time reclining on a sofa waited on by her page
Alphonse: ". . . but if ever an Alphonse carried plain Bill in his
face and figure, that page was the boy".

Mrs. Wititterly (Ch. 21) has a doctor.

> "Your soul is too large for your body", said Mr. Wititterly.
> "Your intellect wears you out; all the medical men say so;
> you know that there is not a physician who is not proud of
> being called in to you. What is their unanimous declara-
> tion?" "My dear doctor", said I to Sir Tumley Snuffim, in
> this very room, the last time he came. "My dear doctor,
> what is my wife's complaint? Tell me all. I can bear it. Is it
> nerves?" "My dear fellow", he said, "be proud of that
> woman; make much of her; she is an ornament to the
> fashionable world, and to you. Her complaint is soul. It
> swells, expands, dilates—the blood fires, the pulse quickens,
> the excitement increases—Whew!"

I like "soul"; under those particular circumstances it was a successful, satisfactory and most salutary diagnosis.

Sir Tumley Snuffim boldly allows Mrs. Wititterly to be the
"first person to take the new medicine which is supposed to have
destroyed a family at Kensington gravelpits". The boldness would
have been all Mrs. Wititterly's if only she had known it. It is
generally wise to avoid new medicines. The gravelpits lay at Not-
ting Hill Gate on the road from London to Oxford, to the east of
Church Lane which became Church Street, where there was also
a brickyard. They were part of the Taplow Terrace, a ridge of
gravel running from Kensington into Essex once marking an an-
cient seashore. There is a fine painting of the Kensington
gravelpits by John Linnell in the Tate Gallery, executed in the
year that Dickens was born. By the 17th century the gravelpits
had become a residential area and the village of Kensington
Gravel Pits was formed. There were some charming houses there
in the 18th century and Queen Anne lived in one of them before
her accession. Tobias Smollett (one of the many medical men who

turned to literature) wrote of the Kensington gravel pits, in *Ferdinand, Count Fathom,* as "the last stage of many a mortal peregrination" anticipating Dickens's morbid reference.

The Kenwigs also have need of a doctor but theirs is not met with until the arrival of their sixth olive branch. They lodge near Golden Square in a faded street where two irregular rows of tall meagre houses seem to have stared each other out of countenance years ago and where thick black smoke pours forth, night and day, from a large brewery hard by. Mr. Kenwigs (Ch. 14) is a turner in ivory who has married above his station but is looked on:

> as a person of some consideration on the premises, inasmuch as he occupied the whole of the first floor, comprising a suite of two rooms.

Mrs. Kenwigs is beautiful and:

> so stately that you would have supposed she had a cook and housemaid at least.

She is quite a lady in her manners and of a very genteel family, having an uncle, Mr. Lillyvick, who collects a water-rate and from whom the family has expectations. The Kenwigs are most agreeable and understandable people, much involved in keeping in with Mr. Lillyvick, a rather delicate business because he is so apt to take sudden offence but can fortunately be induced to calm down again just as rapidly.

Mr. Lillyvick arrives at the party for the Kenwigs' eighth wedding anniversary in a most affable mood to the astonishment of the company for:

> without his book, without his pen and ink, without his double knock, without his intimidation, kissing—actually kissing—an agreeable female, and leaving taxes, summonses, notices that he had called, or announcements that he would never call again, for two quarters' due, wholly out of the question.

There is universal gratification in finding so much humanity in a tax-gatherer. Unfortunately he meets Henrietta Petowker of the

Theatre Royal, Drury Lane at the party who lets down her black hair and recites the Blood-Drinkers' Burial, with the batchelor friend posted in a corner so that he can rush out at the cue "in death expire" and catch her in his arms when she dies raving mad. This performance strikes terror into the hearts of the little Kenwigses but has a rather different effect on the heart of Mr. Lillyvick, who kisses Miss Petowker several times behind the door. However (Ch. 15), the party nearly ends in disaster because the touchy collector

> (the rich relation—the unmarried uncle—who had it in his power to make Morlenna an heiress, and the very baby a legatee—was offended)

becoming angry when Newman Noggs, who (summoned from the party by the arrival of Nicholas and Smike escaping from Dotheboys Hall) seizes a glass of hot punch from under his nose without a word and makes off with it to the relief of his exhausted friends. The Kenwigses are in despair: "Gracious Powers, where was this to end".

Doctor Lumbey is in attendance on the fateful occasion of Mrs. Kenwigs' confinement (Ch. 36) when the Lillyvick disaster is made known:

> He was a stout bluff-looking gentleman, with no shirt collar, to speak of, and a beard that had been growing since yesterday morning; for Doctor Lumbey was popular and the neighbourhood was prolific.

The neighbours agree that:

> there never was such a skilful and scientific doctor as that Doctor Lumbey.

He has the added distinction of being another of Dickens's doctors to be drawn by "Phiz". No wonder he is popular, there he sits, with his hat on, dangling the baby (that is, the old baby—not the new one) on his knee, very much a part of the family gathering, while chaos reigns about him. It is a dramatic moment, Nicholas has just turned up with the awful news that Mr. Lillyvick ("nigh sixty") has married Miss Petowker. The effect on Mr. Kenwigs is terrible:

> "My children, my defrauded, swindled infants!"
> "Villain, ass, traitor!"

The nurse called for silence:

> "Have you no regard for your baby". "No!" returned Mr. Kenwigs. "Let him die", cried Mr. Kenwigs in the torrent of his wrath, "Let him die! He has no expectations, no property to come into. We want no babies here", said Mr. Kenwigs recklessly. "Take 'em away, take 'em away to the Foundling!"

However, all turns out for the best when Henrietta Petowker elopes with a half-pay captain and Mr. Lillyvick "his affections developing themselves in legitimate situations" immediately settles on the Kenwigs' children, when they come of age or marry, that money which he once meant to leave them in his will.

Nicholas Nickleby marks a partial return to the episodic, adventuring style of *Pickwick*, with its young hero whose wanderings lead him into a series of adventures. Nicholas has humour, a sense of the ridiculous and a gay, forceful manner. His mother is one of Dickens's greatest comic characters, and the account of his time, as Mr. Johnson with Crummles' theatricals is superb. This is Dickens in full cry, producing magnificent disorder, crowding his scene with glorious people and overwhelming us with the splendour of his invention. The doctors fit perfectly into the scheme. When reading the greater novels of Dickens's maturity, I find it necessary to reproach myself whenever I detect a lamentable tendency to feel the want of this earlier inspired confusion.

Martin Chuzzlewit (1844)

Martin Chuzzlewit marks a further shift in Dickens's mode of writing; Forster referred to it as the "turning point" in his career. No counterparts to the Kenwigs, Mantalinis or Crummles are to be found even though M. Todgers, in whose breast there was a secret door with "woman" written on the spring, is drawn much in the old style. However, no lovable rogue lurks beneath the Pecksniff villainy and his daughters are so harshly treated that they allow no family humour to develop and enchant us as it does in *Nicholas Nickleby*. *Martin Chuzzlewit* is a dramatic and tragic tale on the theme of how selfishness may warp and ruin men's lives driving them to desperate deeds, and of how self-denial and large-hearted benevolence may triumph over disaster. The doctors, in keeping with this development and unlike their predecessors, are neither efficient, agreeable, foolish nor full of fun. Bob Sawyer occupied a joyously recurring place in the light-hearted adventures of *Pickwick Papers;* Mr. Losberne bustled about taking care of his patients and arranging everything he could in the latter half of *Oliver Twist;* and Lumley and Snuffim happily enlivened minor episodes in *Nicholas Nickleby;* but John Jobling and young Lewsome play far deeper and more sinister roles in *Martin Chuzzlewit*. They occupy important places in the main stream of the story; they are concerned in a swindle and a murder.

The nurses, Sarah Gamp and Betsy Prig, are horrifying examples of the one-time state of the nursing profession. Dickens wrote in the preface: "Mrs. Sarah Gamp was, four-and-twenty years ago, a fair representation of the hired attendant on the poor in sickness". When *Martin Chuzzlewit* was published Florence Nightingale was 24 years of age; she was then visiting hospitals and reformatories in Europe but ten years were to pass before she would go to the Crimea and 12 before her Nurses Training School was to be established at St. Thomas's Hospital.

Sarah Gamp remains unique: she was instrumental in arousing the public conscience to the need for nursing reform and, at the same time, is one of the greatest comic creations in all literature. She could have achieved such eminence alone but her right to it was doubly established by the stroke of genius which inspired the invention of Mrs. Harris to enhance her humour. Each time I re-read Betsy Prig's terrible words: "I don't believe there's no sich a person!", I feel that this awful statement requires a voice like that of Edith Evans to do it justice; "lambs could not forgive, nor worms forget!"

There are two minor doctors in the American part of *Martin Chuzzlewit*. I used to skip this American episode when I was young, but it is there that Martin sheds his family inheritance of selfishness under the influence of Mark Tapley and this part of the story grows on you. Soon after his arrival Martin meets a kindly man, Dr. Bevan, "his profession was physic, though he seldom or never practised". At the end of his stay when he is starting on his journey home, Martin meets The Honourable Elijah Pogram, Member of Congress, who had delivered the oration known as the Pogram Defiance (Ch. 34) which:

> Defied the world in general to com-pete with our country upon any hook; and devellop'd our internal resources for making war upon the universal airth.

Pogram, a great artist in the characteristic political skill of twisting other people's words to support his own ends, is given a levee at the National Hotel. The deputation which waits on him to announce this honour consists of six boarders and a very shrill boy. The spokesman of the group is Doctor Ginery Dunkle, a gentleman of great poetical elements. When it is all over he:

> immediately repaired to the newspaper-office, and there wrote a short poem suggested by the events of the evening, beginning with fourteen stars, and headed, "A Fragment. Suggested by witnessing the Honourable Elijah Pogram

engaged in a philosophical disputation with three of Columbia's fairest daughters. By Doctor Ginery Dunkle of Troy".

Doctor John Jobling (also illustrated by "Phiz") has a recurring influence on the life of Jonas Chuzzlewit. We meet him first newly arrived at the death bed of Anthony Chuzzlewit, whom he bleeds and to whom he applies other remedies while totally unaware of the fact that Jonas has attempted to poison him. Dr. Jobling is also to be found attending a young man, housed at the Bull in Holborn, who seems to be dying but manages to cheat Mr. Mould the undertaker (who refers to him as: "The gentleman that Mrs. Gamp thought likely to suit us"). The doctor says that the fever must take its course and shakes his head: "It was all he could do under the circumstances and he did it well". This is the one point in the story which brings the two doctors together for the patient, an old school fellow of John Westlock's whose ramblings in delirium are overheard by Mrs. Gamp, turns out to be Lewsome.

When we next meet Doctor Jobling, a gentleman has done him the honour of making a very handsome mention of him in his will in testimony of his unremitting zeal, talent and attention. He has been appointed as Medical Officer to the Anglo-Bengalee Disinterested Loan and Life Assurance Company run by Montague Tigg Esquire (of Pall Mall and Bengal), is in a jovial mood (Ch. 27) and has obviously become a success:

> He had a portentously sagacious chin, and a pompous voice, with a rich huskiness in some of its tones that went directly to the heart, like a ray of light shining through the ruddy medium of choice old burgundy. . . . Perhaps he could shake his head, rub his hands, or warm himself before a fire, better than any man alive; and he had a peculiar way of smacking his lips and saying, "Ah!" at intervals while patients detailed their symptoms, which inspired great confidence.

We can almost see him at it; I have had cause to admire the way in which some physicians get away with saying nothing of any consequence either to the patient or to his relatives.

Jobling is useful in introducing patients to the company (on commission) from among the tradesmen and their families which he attends but is far too knowing to connect himself with the business in any way except as a well-paid functionary, covering any risk to himself from his laudation by telling his patients that he is bound to speak well of the establishment which employs him. He is responsible for introducing Jonas to Anglo-Bengalee and so to the swindle and blackmail which brings him to the premeditated murder of Montague Tigg. Doctor Jobling greets the chairman of Anglo-Bengalee with:

> "And how are *you*, Mr. Montague, eh? . . . A little worn with business eh? If so, rest. A little feverish with wine, humph? If so, water. Nothing at all the matter, and quite comfortable? Then take some lunch. A very wholesome thing at this time of day to strengthen the gastric juices with lunch, Mr. Montague . . . I always take it myself about this time of day, do you know!"

He then uses Mr. Crimple's leg to demonstrate how the neglect of meals causes the animal oils in the knee joint to wane and become exhausted so that Mr. Crimple's bones will sink down into their sockets and Mr. Crimple (who in fact makes off with the money when Montague Tigg is murdered) will become a:

> weazen, puny, stunted, miserable man! . . . "We know a few secrets of nature in our profession, sir. Of course we do. We study for that; we pass the Hall and the College for that; and we take our station in society *by* that."

Lunching with Jonas in the Medical Officer's own room, after he has been properly hooked, the doctor takes a case of lancets out of his pocket before starting to eat ("My pockets are rather tight. Ha, ha, ha!") to Jonas's great interest. He enquires about their sharpness and suitability for opening a vein and about the exact location of the jugular, but gets more than he hoped for when he is given details of a murder committed by a member of the medical profession—most artistically done, stabbed to the heart and only one drop of blood. The doctor's last words as Jonas

and Montague Tigg start out on their fateful journey are "It will
be a stormy night!"

Doctor Lewsome (Ch. 25) is:

> a young man—dark and not ill-looking—with long black
> hair,

of whom Mrs. Gamp said he'd make a lovely corpse. He recovers
from his fever and is taken into

> Har'fordshire, which is his native air

by Mrs. Gamp and handed over to a

> country nuss (drat them country nusses, much the orkard
> hussies knows about their bis'ness).

He recovers and returns to tell John Westlock the story of how, as
an assistant to a surgeon in the City, he had met Jonas
Chuzzlewit, lost money to him gaming and been induced to
procure the poison for him to murder his father. He denounces
Jonas at the end only to learn from Chuffey that Anthony
Chuzzlewit had discovered the plot, destroyed the poison and
died a natural death leaving Jonas to believe that he had killed
him. There is, however, no escape for Jonas who commits suicide
when apprehended for the murder of Montague Tigg.

The Battle of Life (1846)

The public, which had clamoured for *The Old Curiosity Shop* (1841) and delighted to weep for little Nell and to revel in the evil Guilp, had not been overwhelmed with *Barnaby Rudge* (1841) and did not, at first, care much for *Martin Chuzzlewit.* When it began to appear there was "a grave depreciation of sale in his writings" (Forster). It was temporary but disturbing. *Martin Chuzzlewit*first appeared in serial form in January 1843 and, in his spare moments between producing the monthly parts, Dickens decided to try to recover his waning finances and meet the growing demands of his family by writing a book for Christmas. To most writers the idea of finding spare moments for creation at such a time, and of adding yet another dead-line that must be met, would seem incredible. Nevertheless, *A Christmas Carol* appeared in time for Christmas 1843, the parts of *Martin Chuzzlewit* continued to come out until June 1844, and the second Christmas book, *The Chimes,* was ready by December 1844. Today with our tardy publishing it seems hardly less remarkable that Chapman and Hall, Dickens's publishers up to that time, should be producing all those books, on time and at such short notice. In 1845 Dickens wrote *The Cricket on the Hearth* for Christmas and in 1846 started *Dombey and Son,* producing *The Battle of Life* as the Christmas book that year.

There is only one doctor of medicine in the Christmas books. This doctor is Alfred Heathfield (a ward of the philosopher Doctor Jeddler who is a widower), a handsome young medical student who, at the start of the story, is about to leave for three years' study in foreign schools of medicine. He is in love with the younger of Doctor Jeddler's two daughters, both of whom are in love with him. He returns on a stormy Christmas night to find that his love has fled with Michael Warden. He later marries the elder sister and settles down to run the local practice. Six years after her departure the younger sister returns to explain that she has been living with an aunt, never eloped with Michael Warden but went away, although she loved Alfred, solely to leave the field clear for her beloved sister to whom she owed so much. Not much of a Christmas tale for my choice although the early part has charm and contains some good characters: Clemency Newcome, a homely, capable, sensible girl who ends up running both "The Nutmeg-grater and Thimble" and her husband without him knowing it, and the lawyers, Craggs and Snitchey, close friends and true partners, each of whose wives is convinced that her husband is being exploited by the other.

I never cared very much for Scrooge, the ghost, the spirits or his conversion when I was young. So slight a wavering in devotion to all that Dickens wrote may perhaps be forgiven. Dickens, in the preface to the collected edition of *Christmas Books* published in 1852 wrote:

> "My chief purpose was, in a whimsical kind of masque which the good humour of the season justified, to awaken some loving and forbearing thoughts, never out of season in a Christian land".

This blind spot of mine makes it hard for me to understand, even with the help of most loving and forbearing thoughts, how many people who failed to appreciate *Martin Chuzzlewit,* were so easily revived in loyalty by *A Christmas Carol,* which, nevertheless, deservedly remains a great public favourite. *The Battle of Life* with its disappointed doctor who marries the wrong girl may perhaps make the other Christmas books seem brighter or is it comparison with the stupendous march of the great novels that unfairly diminishes the lesser intention of *Christmas Books.*

Dombey and Son (1848)

The public came back in their thousands to buy the first numbers of *Dombey and Son,* Dickens was himself again in their eyes. The two doctors it contains are once more, in the old less important roles, in glorious form. The first number, which contained them both, went off (Ch. 1) in style:

> Dombey sat in the corner of the darkened room in the great arm-chair by the bedside, and Son lay tucked up warm in a little basket bedstead, carefully disposed on a low settee immediately in front of the fire and close to it, as if his constitution were analogous to that of a muffin, and it was essential to toast him brown while he was very new. Dombey was about eight-and-forty years of age. Son about eight-and-forty minutes.

The birth is attended by Doctor Parker Peps:

> one of the Court Physicians, and a man of immense reputation for assisting at the increase of great families.

He walks up and down with his hands behind him, to the unspeakable admiration of the family surgeon, Mr. Pilkins, who has been telling all his patients, friends and acquaintances for the last six weeks that he is in hourly expectation of being summoned in conjunction with Doctor Parker Peps. The third attendant is Mrs. Blockitt the nurse:

> a simpering piece of faded gentility, who did not presume to state her name as a fact, but merely offered it as a mild suggestion.

Dombey descends to speak with the doctors about his son:

"Well, Sir", said Doctor Parker Peps in a round, deep, sonorous voice, muffled for the occasion, like the knocker; "do you find that your dear lady, is at all roused by your visit?"

"Stimulated as it were?" said the family practitioner faintly: bowing at the same time to the Doctor, as much as to say, "Excuse my putting in a word, but this is a valuable connexion."

Mr. Dombey was quite discomforted by the question. He had thought so little of the patient, that he was not in a condition to answer it.

Parker Peps, who gave notice both of the extent of his practice and of its class by carefully confusing the names of his patients, having referred to Mrs. Dombey as Lady Cankaby and the Countess of Dombey, warned Mr. Dombey:

"that there is a want of power in Her Grace the Duchess — I beg your pardon; I confuse names; I should say, in your amiable lady. That there is a certain degree of languor, and a general absence of elasticity."

When Mr. Dombey goes up later to see his wife the situation is grave. There is a solemn stillness round the bed; the two medical attendants are looking on the impassive form with much compassion and little hope. So the first Mrs. Dombey dies.

Doctor Parker Peps, later to become Sir Parker, is well known to many of us. There were several fine examples of Peps around when I was a medical student, though they are not so common to-day. I still know one physician, however, who is apt if not to confuse his dukes at least to drop their names from time to time and thus inspire the deepest respect, but he is, nevertheless, an outstandingly good doctor. The vague relative who seems unable to accept the seriousness of an illness in a loved one is usually shutting his mind to an unacceptable situation and is disconcertingly liable to complain later on that he was never properly informed. The lofty indifference of Mr. Dombey, however, is genuine and is beautifully described:

He was not a man of whom it could properly be said that he was never startled or shocked; but he certainly had a sense within him, that if his wife should sicken and decay, he would be very sorry, and that he would find a something gone from among his plate and furniture, and other household possessions, which was well worth the having, and could not be lost without sincere regret. Though it would be a cool, business-like, gentlemanly, self-possessed regret, no doubt.

A few years later the young Paul asks his father what money is, and gets, by way of an answer, that it can *do* anything, he then surprises his father by broaching the subject of his mother for the first time and speculating on why money didn't save her. This puts Mr. Dombey (Ch. 8) in some difficulty:

> He expounded to him how that money, though a very potent spirit, never to be disparaged on any account whatever, could not keep people alive whose time was come to die; and how that we must all die, unfortunately, even in the City, though we were never so rich. But how that money caused us to be honoured, feared, respected, courted, and admired, and made us powerful and glorious in the eyes of all men; and how that it could, very often, even keep off death, for a long time together. How, for example, it had secured to his Mama the services of Mr. Pilkins, by which he, Paul, had often profited himself; likewise of the great Doctor Parker Peps, whom he had never known.

Paul does get to know Parker Peps, however. When he begins to ail, Mr. Pilkins sends him to the sea where he is seen at Mr. Blimbers' establishment by a certain calm apothecary who attends the school. He is never destined to live, however, and as he fails he is visited by three grave doctors. Paul's interest centres on Sir Parker Peps, who always took his seat on the side of the bed. Two of the medical attendants are at the funeral, presumably not Sir Parker who would most assuredly have been mentioned by name had he been there.

There is one excellent therapeutic suggestion put forward in *Dombey and Son* when Solomon Gills is off his food and Walter tells him that he will have to bring a doctor to him if he goes on like that. Sol (Ch. 9) answers:

> "He can't give me what I want, my boy. At least he is in good practice if he can—and then he wouldn't."
> "What is it, Uncle? Customers?"
> "Aye", returned Solomon, with a sigh, "customers would do."

Dombey and Son is such an astonishing display of the creative art that you feel ungrateful for wanting something more. It is a spectacular success but enchanted acclaim is tempered with some regret. Dombey himself is wonderfully drawn, but whatever did he *do* in that business? He neglects his wife and rejects his daughter, the only two to offer him love, and concentrates on the son who is to follow him as a producer of wealth and an employer of power. The travesty of an education which he designs to achieve this end and his failure in human relationships lead to a personal tragedy. Paul's early departure and the slow build up of Dombey's relationship with Florence leaves the centre of the stage to two improbable characters with an unrealistic relationship. James Carker seems a poor villain who, like the Cheshire cat, leaves nothing much behind him but a grin. The second Mrs. Dombey is a remarkable, controlled and tormented woman full of suppressed force but is involved in so many complications that she never quite achieves probability, or rises to the stature of Lady Dedlock.

The doctors come in the better half of the book; Susan Nipper, Joe Bagstock, Captain Cuttle and Toots continue to give delight but the second half never quite comes up to the first. The doctors are Dombey men; their services are secured by wealth and they respond with a finely calculated blend of flattery and conceit. They play into each others hands, promote their importance and reveal no trace of warmth, concern or indeed genuine feeling of any kind, matters which Mr. Dombey would certainly not have understood. They suit him down to the ground.

David Copperfield (1850)

David Copperfield is acknowledged to be one of the greatest of Dickens's novels. It was written at the height of his powers, it contains more elements of autobiography than the others, and, of all his works, was Dickens's own favourite. The fact that it is written in the first person was thought by J. B. Priestley to have much to do with Dickens's preference. An author who tells a tale in the words of his principal character tends to acquire a peculiar and particularly affectionate intimacy with the story. We know from the preface to *David Copperfield* that at the close of the two years imaginative task involved in its creation, Dickens was sad to be separated from so many companions. "No one", he wrote, "can ever believe this Narrative, in the reading, more than I believed it in the writing."

It is a wonderful story, one of the most carefully planned of Dickens's novels, deeply involved with society, highly perceptive of the feelings of the young and containing for good measure, the unforgettable Mr. and Mrs. Micawber and that wonderful great-aunt Betsy Trotwood. On re-reading, it is of all the novels the one which recalls most vividly my feelings on first hearing it read as a child. A story can be more real to the young than all the humdrum reality around them. There is then no thought of making allowances for actions, of seeing shades of character, of permitting excuses or of entertaining qualifications, people are only lovable or hateful. To me Mr. Murdstone was then a truly fearsome character, larger and blacker than he is today, the personification of tyranny, whose domination was made the more complete by his stony-hearted sister. Similarly my fear of Mr. Creakle was enhanced by the presence of Tungay, with his wooden leg, bull-neck, and close cut hair, who repeated Mr.

Creakle's threats and regarded the whole establishment of Salem House, masters and boys, as his natural enemies. Peggotty made life bearable through the early chapters before relief came with Betsey Trotwood's confrontation of Mr. Murdstone and, at last, with Mr. Micawber's exposure of Uriah Heep. As with none of the other novels, I can today experience once again some of my intensity of feeling on first hearing *The Personal History of David Copperfield*, even while responding with calmer enjoyment to more subtle blends of character. Only Rosa Dartle, bitter, ruthless, disfigured and the very embodiment of malevolence, retains for me all her old uncomplicated venom. Dickens should first be read when young.

There is not a great deal to be heard of doctors in *David Copperfield* but, as in *Oliver Twist* and in *Dombey and Son*, we start with a birth and Mr. Chillip is early on the scene. Mrs. Copperfield, Peggotty and her nephew Ham (secreted in the house as a special messenger in case of emergency) and Betsy Trotwood are the only people who get into the story before him. Mr. Chillip (Ch. 1) was:

> the meekest of his sex, the mildest of little men. He sidled in and out of a room, to take up the less space. He walked as softly as the Ghost in Hamlet, and more slowly. He carried his head on one side, partly in modest depreciation of himself, partly in modest propitiation of everybody else. It is nothing to say that he hadn't a word to throw at a dog. He couldn't have *thrown* a word at a mad dog. He might have offered him one gently, or half a one, or a fragment of one; for he spoke as slowly as he walked; but he wouldn't have been rude to him, and he couldn't have been quick with him, for any earthly consideration.

He has a marvellous conversation with Miss Betsey who keeps her ears plugged with wadges of jewellers' cotton, pulls them out like corks to hear him and promptly stops them up again. Waiting, in her company, for progress to occur upstairs nearly breaks his spirit and he spends the last part of the ordeal sitting on the stairs in the dark and a strong draught rather than face her any longer.

Eventually, when all is over, he has to break the terrible news to her that it is a boy, whereupon she aims a blow at his head with her bonnet, walks out, and never comes back. Once she has appreciated the enormity of the fact that the child is not to be called Betsey Trotwood Copperfield "she vanished like a discontented fairy". Later recollecting the occasion (Ch. 13) she says:

> "That little man of a doctor, with his head on one side, Jellips, or whatever his name was, what was *he* about? All he could do was to say to me, like a robin redbreast — as he *is* — 'It's a boy'. A boy! Yah, the imbecility of the whole set of 'em!"

while many years later Mr. Chillip (Ch. 59) admits:

> "it was some time before I recovered the conduct of that alarming lady, on the night of your birth, Mr. Copperfield".

David is born in a caul which is advertised for sale, in the newspapers, at the low price of fifteen guineas. Cauls were then being sold for as much as £30, a considerable sum in the middle of the nineteenth century. For David's caul (Ch. 1) there is but a solitary bidder:

> an attorney connected with the bill-broking business, who offered two pounds in cash, and the balance in sherry, but declined to be guaranteed from drowning on any higher bargain.

This offer is refused and ten years later the caul is put up in a raffle (by whom I wonder?) and is won by an old lady long remembered as remarkable in that:

> she was never drowned, but died triumphantly in bed, at ninety-two

having never been on the water in her life. The superstition of the lucky caul and its power to prevent death by drowning was commonly held from early times. St. Chrysostom (golden-mouth), born in Antioch in A.D. 347, used his splendid eloquence, in his homilies, to denounce belief in the magic of the caul. *The Times* was still carrying advertisements for the sale of cauls when Dickens was writing *David Copperfield*. Did he introduce this superstition at the very start of the story as an ominous herald of the drownings to come?

It is possible that "Phiz" drew a picture of Mr. Chillip though I think he did not. There is a picture of David and his mother in their pew in one of "Phiz's" curious churches, which it would take an ecclesiastical architect to unravel, like The Little Church in the Park in *Bleak House*. This one (probably taken from St Mary's, Chatham) shows many members of the congregation: Mr. Murdstone is there, easily distinguished with his black whiskers, leaning with his elbow on a pew which has a door with a key in the lock, looking at Mrs. Copperfield. David (Ch. 2) looks around and his mind wanders:

> I look at my mother, but *she* pretends not to see me. I look at a boy in the aisle, and *he* makes faces at me. I look at the sunlight coming in at the open door through the porch, and there I see a stray sheep—I don't mean a sinner, but mutton—half making up his mind to come into the church. I feel that if I looked at him any longer, I might be tempted to say something out loud; and what would become of me then! I look up at the monumental tablets on the wall, and try to think of Mr. Bodgers late of this parish, and what the feelings of Mrs. Bodgers must have been, when affliction sore, long time Mr. Bodgers bore, and physicians were in vain. I wonder whether they called in Mr. Chillip, and he was in vain; and if so, how he likes to be reminded of it once a week. I look from Mr. Chillip, in his Sunday neckcloth, to the pulpit; and think what a good place it would be to play in, and what a castle it would make, with another boy coming up the stairs to attack it, and having the velvet cushion with the tassels thrown down on his head.

But where is Mr. Chillip and should we expect to see Mrs. Chillip there with him? There are not many to choose from, for most of the people in the picture sit behind David and are out of his view. My reading of the matter is that the Chillips are not in the picture but share with us the sheep's eye view from the north transept — or can it be the south transept judged by the position of the font in this unusual church?

Mr. Chillip is a kindly man and a comfort to David after his mother's death. It is reported of him (Ch. 30) that, when attending the death bed of Mr. Barkis:

> Mr. Chillip had mournfully said in the kitchen, on going away just now, that the College of Physicians, the College of Surgeons, and Apothecaries' Hall, if they were all called in together, couldn't help him. He was past both Colleges, Mr. Chillip said, and the Hall could only poison him.

Mr. Chillip's family life is not easy to follow: he became a widower some years before David left Salem House, at which time David was going on for 10 years of age, having lost his small light-haired wife whom David could just remember and connected in his thoughts with a pale tortoise-shell cat. By the time of Mr. Barkis' funeral, when David was a young man just before Emily ran away with Steerforth, Mr. Chillip must have remarried since his baby "wagged its heavy head, and rolled its goggle-eyes at the clergyman over its nurse's shoulder". When David is famous, after he comes back from his long trip abroad following Dora's death, he meets Mr. Chillip again "tolerably stricken in years" whose daughter is then quite a tall lass: "Her mother let down two tucks in her frocks only last week".

Both Mr. Spenlow and Dora die of natural causes without benefit of doctors, unless "they" who keep telling David things are doctors. Doctors, however, attend Mrs. Steerforth when she is prostrated by news of James' death by drowning. But Mr. Chillip is the only doctor to appear in *David Copperfield* by name, he is one of the first there and he comes back at the end of the book to help tie up loose ends, especially to give his news of the Murdstones. The second Mrs. Chillip (who came into some property near Bury St. Edmunds under her father's will) being a great observer, notes the way in which the Murdstones have once again broken the spirit of a young wife "with a very good little property, poor thing".

The last news of Wilkins Micawber is the account in the *Port Middlebay Times* of the public dinner in his honour presided over by Doctor Mell who turns out to be Charles Mell the teacher at Salem House, dismissed because his mother lived in an almshouse. He has made good in Australia and being a school teacher has presumably acquired his doctorate in some suitable academic subject.

Bleak House (1853)

In the previous novels doctors had either appeared in their own right as gloriously magnified, early-style Dickensian characters, like Sir Tumley Snuffim and Sir Parker Peps, or had played important roles in the evolution of the story, like Mr. Losberne and Dr. Jobling. In *Bleak House* much is changed. It contains a fascinatingly contrasted trio of doctors but, rather surprisingly, in what is a far more closely woven story than any that has gone before, they fit less snugly into either of the old categories. They stand curiously aloof from the drama. Mr. Bayham Badger makes a brief and delightful appearance and is the nearest of the three to an old-style Dickens character. Mr. Skimpole is irrelevant to the plot which could have unfolded quite well without him, but his conversation is so entrancing and his behaviour so infuriating that he creates an unforgettable impression. Dr. Allan Woodcourt also keeps coming into the story without producing any noticeable effect on the grave affairs being enacted around him.

The huge success of *David Copperfield* led to an even larger subscription list for *Bleak House*. This is a most serious work, more mature and, despite its complexity, better organised than any of its predecessors. A magnificent book confirming Dickens's claim to be one of the very greatest of all novelists, full of character and effective attacks on the evils of the social and legal systems of the day. However, much of the extravagance, a good deal of the fun, some of the gusto and that breath of innocence, warmth and geniality which had done so much to win Dickens his large following, are missing. It also lacks a central character; there is no-one to mind about all the time. The centre of the stage is taken by two main themes rather than by a hero and a heroine: these are the tragedy of Lady Dedlock's secret and the corrupting

influence of the long drawn out Chancery suit. The planning and
the style have come a long way from *Pickwick Papers,* the
characters are here bound together in an intricate web of events,
in which chance, coincidence, a bundle of letters and even a
handkerchief all play their carefully chosen parts. It is, therefore,
all the more surprising that the doctors should seem so remote.
Many threads are held by quite minor characters: Trooper
George, for example, runs a shooting gallery and teaches fencing
to Richard Carstone, but turns out to be the son of the
housekeeper at Chesney Wold, the brother of the ironmaster Mr.
Rouncewell, to be in debt to old Smallweed, to have served under
Captain Hawdon and able to supply a specimen of his handwriting to Mr. Tulkinghorn and ends up as attendant to the shat-
tered Sir Leicester Dedlock.

Bleak House starts with the famous description of a London fog
to set the stage for the gloomy scenes to follow; the whole novel is
pervaded by a sense of doom enhanced by a mounting emphasis
on the inescapable consequences of past deeds. The general effect
is magnificent. There are, however, less people to love than the
devotees had come to expect despite a marvellous assembly of
characters such as Mrs. Jellyby, Mr. Turveydrop, Mr. Chadband,
Mr. Tulkinghorn, Jo, and those superb Dedlocks. There are a few
glaring improbabilities which pale beside the grand improbabili-
ty that this mighty concept could ever have been brought to such
a triumphant conclusion. Perfection could not have been half so
engaging—and yet, I miss the instant friends of simpler days.

When Richard Carstone is launched on the first of his brief and
abortive attempts to embrace a profession, his medical studies are
guided by Mr. Bayham Badger, a cousin of "Conversation"
Kenge, John Jarndyce's solicitor. Mr. Badger practises in Chelsea
and attends a large public Institution. Which one I wonder? Mr.
Boythorn, of whom, Harold Skimpole (Ch. 15) said:

> "Nature forgot to shade him off, I think? A little too
> boisterous—like the sea? A little too vehement—like a bull,
> who has made up his mind to consider every colour scarlet?
> But, I grant a sledge-hammering sort of merit in him!"

makes a comment on Richard's medical studies (Ch. 13), which
our formerly grossly underpaid junior doctors who responded
with inappropriate demands to be paid for overtime work, the
just reward of those without responsibility, might have used with
more force to support their claim for better pay when confronting
the Minister of Health:

> "I rejoice to find a young gentleman of spirit and gallan-
> try devoting himself to that noble profession! The more
> spirit there is in it, the better for mankind, and the worse for
> those mercenary task-masters and low tricksters who delight
> in putting that illustrious art at a disadvantage in the world
> . . . — as to those fellows, who meanly take advantage of the
> ardour of gentlemen in the pursuit of knowledge, to
> recompense the inestimable services of the best years of their
> lives, their long study, and their expensive education, with
> pittances too small for the acceptance of clerks, I would
> have the necks of every one of them wrung, and the skulls ar-
> ranged in Surgeons' Hall for the contemplation of the whole
> profession — in order that its younger members might
> understand from actual measurement, in early life, *how*
> thick skulls may become."

Bayham Badger is soon disposed of, but Dickens gives us, in
passing (Ch. 13), one of his characteristic, throw-away sketches:

> Mr. Bayham Badger himself a pink, fresh-faced, crisp-
> looking gentleman, with a weak voice, white teeth, light
> hair, and surprised eyes: some years younger, I should say,
> than Mrs. Bayham Badger

takes a special delight in being Mrs. Badger's third. He proudly
displays the portraits of Captain Swosser of the Royal Navy, Mrs.
Badger's first, and of Professor Dingo of European reputation,
Mrs. Badger's second, to John Jarndyce watched, in "Phiz's" illustration, by Mrs. Badger, Ada, Esther and Richard. He is
delighted to have followed such distinguished predecessors and
proud that Mrs. Badger did not have:

> the appearance of a lady who has had two former husbands.

Dr. Alan Woodcourt slides so unobtrusively into the story that it is some time before we know his name. He turns out to be a serious young doctor in a busy general practice whose well directed attentions and practical ability stand in contrast to the misdirected energies of those philanthropists, Mrs. Jellyby whose charity begins abroad and Mrs. Pardiggle whose condescension to the poor is so offensive. The one redeeming thing about Mrs. Pardiggle's cruel imposition on her children, by which she forces them to donate their pocket money to charity, is her decision that Oswald, her ten-and-a-half year old second, shall give his two-and-ninepence to the cause of the Great National Smithers Testimonial, now sadly in abeyance. A few such are with us still. I have met a famous lady, immersed in charity, in frail command of a battalion of devoted helpers which she rules with little regard for their (or indeed for her own) hours of sleep or family life, to whom I am apt to refer with only mild injustice, as Mrs. Jellyby. Alan Woodcourt is really there to marry Esther Summerson, take her off to Yorkshire and save her from a fate, which for her sweet, coy and positively tender spitefulness she so richly deserves. Without him she would have married old John Jarndyce and forever gone about her depressing Dame Durden duties carrying a basket containing two bunches of housekeeping keys — all labelled.

Poor Allan Woodcourt, one of Dickens's good doctors, is so dull and has so little spirit that he has to go away to sea and become the hero of a pointless shipwreck, off stage, to acquire some substance. His first appearance is as "a dark young man" (the only description he is vouchsafed by the greatest of all masters of pen portraiture), who relieves "a testy medical man, brought from his dinner — with a broad snuffy upper lip and a broad Scotch tongue", who announces that Nemo (one of Mr. Snagsby's copy-writers who turns out to be Esther's father, Captain Hawdon) "Wull have been dead aboot three hours". This is one of the crucial points in the story because Mr. Tulkinghorn is there following up his first clue to Lady Dedlock's secret, offered to his sharp notice when her interest is suddenly aroused by recognising Nemo's handwriting on a legal document to the extent that a slight disturbance could be observed in her habitual calm.

Mr. Krook, the landlord,is there to start another train of events in the mounting attack on Lady Dedlock's past by dying and so handing on to his brother-in-law, the usurer Mr. Smallweed, the bundle of letters found in the dead man's portmanteau. Miss Flite, the other lodger, is there to link the destruction of Lady Dedlock with the apparently interminable case of Jarndyce v. Jarndyce. The young surgeon, however, is only there to be introduced and to diagnose that the cause of death was an overdose of opium which, curiously to our ears, he claimed that the deceased had purchased from him regularly over the past year and a half.

Allan Woodcourt makes his next appearance as a guest at the dinner party given by the Bayham Badgers after Richard has been accepted as a pupil but we do not know that he has been there until it is all over and even then we have still to learn his name. He is merely "a young surgeon" coyly referred to by Esther (Ch. 13) in her most irritating manner:

> I have omitted to mention in its place, that there was someone else at the family dinner party. It was not a lady. It was a gentleman. It was a gentleman of a dark complexion—a young surgeon. He was rather reserved, but I thought him very sensible and agreeable. At least, Ada asked me if I did not, and I said yes.

Later Alan Woodcourt befriends Richard Carstone but is unable to prevent his steady decline. Richard gives up everything to a pursuit of false hopes of a legacy from Jarndyce v. Jarndyce which leads to his death when he finds that the whole estate has been absorbed in legal costs.

By far the most interesting doctor in *Bleak House* is Harold Skimpole, who has to be included in any list of Dickens's doctors for his delightful conversation even if his medical practice (Ch. 6) was confined to having once lived, in his professional capacity, in the household of a German Prince.

> He was a little bright creature, with a rather large head; but a delicate face, and a sweet voice, and there was a

perfect charm in him. All he said was so free from effort and
spontaneous, and was said with such a captivating gaiety,
that it was fascinating to hear him talk. . . . Indeed he had
more the appearance, in all respects, of a damaged young
man, than a well-preserved elderly one. There was an easy
negligence in his manner, and even in his dress (his hair
carelessly disposed, and his neck-kerchief loose and flowing,
as I have seen artists paint their own portraits), which I
could not separate from the idea of a romantic youth who
had undergone some unique process of depreciation.

Mr. Skimpole's exquisite conversation is brilliantly presented, it
flows naturally, has delicate little twists, and is altogether so
charming that you find yourself turning back to read each of his
little speeches (Ch. 8) all over again.

Mr. Skimpole was as agreeable at breakfast, as he had
been over-night. There was honey on the table, and it led
him into a discourse about Bees. He had no objection to
honey, he said, . . . but he protested against the overween-
ing assumptions of Bees. He didn't at all see why the busy
Bee should be proposed as a model to him; he supposed the
Bee liked to make honey, or he wouldn't do it — nobody asked him. It was not necessary for the Bee to make a merit of
his tastes. If every confectioner went buzzing about the
world, banging against everything that came in his way, and
egotistically calling upon everybody to take notice that he
was going to his work and must not be interrupted, the
world would be quite an unsupportable place.

Eugene Wrayburn also protested, though less elegantly, on being
referred to the bees as an example and a guide to conduct, object-
ing on principle, as a biped, to being required to model his proceedings according to those of a bee.

Harold Skimpole told the bailiff's daughter (Ch. 37) with a
patriarchial air:

that he had given her late father the business in his power;
and that if one of her little brothers would make haste to get

set-up in the same profession, he hoped he should still be able to put a good deal of employment in his way.

"For I am constantly being taken in these nets", said Mr. Skimpole, looking beamingly at us over a glass of wine-and-water, "and am constantly being bailed out—like a boat. Or paid off—like a ship's company. Somebody always does it for me. *I* can't do it, you know, for I have never had any money."

Mr. Skimpole's irresponsibility and childishness are surely taken to extremes when (Ch. 15) he says to his own doctor:

"Now, my dear doctor, it is quite a delusion on your part to suppose that you attend me for nothing. I am overwhelming you with money—in my expansive intentions—if you only knew it!"

Dickens based Mr. Skimpole on Leigh Hunt, essayist, poet and friend of Byron, Keats and Shelley, who was introduced to him by John Forster and had been one of the people considered to write the text for those illustrations of Robert Seymour's which led to *Pickwick Papers*. Leigh Hunt wrote of that first encounter: "What a face is his to meet in a drawing room! It has the life and soul in it of fifty human beings". If Mr. Skimpole started out as Leigh Hunt he must soon have taken off in his own right. I imagine that Dickens, however charming a companion he had at first created, began to lose his affection for this gay scrounger and wilful drop-out. His feelings for him seem to have soured as Skimpole's weaknesses and lack of heart became more obvious under the scrutiny of Esther's sweet brand of malevolence and as the story allowed him diminishing opportunity to display his brilliant conversation.

Esther has no use for Skimpole, she spitefully reports his sayings in her sweetest manner and ceases to think him artless, believing that his avowal of weakness and display of guileless candour are only there to serve his idle turn and to see that he has the least trouble. When he becomes involved in serious matters he can adopt a sensible attitude but does so with such timidity, lack of heart and furtive dealing that it saps our tolerance and leads

Esther to call it treachery. He advises them to turn Jo from the house when he arrives with smallpox, and when they refuse he prescribes cooling medicine, sprinkling vinegar about the place where he sleeps and keeping it moderately cool and him moderately warm. But he then conspires behind Mr. Jarndyce's back to have the boy removed next day (taking £5 off Mr. Bucket in the process) but not before Charley has caught the infection which she is to hand on to Esther so that her face becomes scarred and her beauty frayed. Mr. Bucket is a remarkable man worthy of a detective novel all his own, a better man than Sergeant Cuff, the detective created by Dickens's friend Wilkie Collins. Bucket sums up Skimpole when he says he has "no idea of money. He takes it though!"

Forster tells a charming story of Leigh Hunt who asked the Duke of Devonshire for a loan of £200 for two years, owing to a delay in the production of his first play: "the duke replied by taking the money himself to Hunt's house in Edwarde Square. On the last day of the second year within which repayment was promised, Hunt (quite out of character as Mr. Skimpole) sent back the £200; and was startled, the morning after, by another visit from the duke, who pressed upon him its reacceptance as a gift. He added that there would be no obligation for he was himself Hunt's debtor. He was ill when asked for the loan, and it had done him good to comply with the request. Never but once before had borrowed money ever come back to him, and he should always retain the sense of pleasure which its return had occasioned."

Little Dorrit (1857)

Little Dorrit is a sad and rather sombre tale. It starts in one prison moves on to another and is throughout concerned with constraint. William Dorrit spends twenty years in the Marshalsea, where Dickens's father was once imprisoned for debt. Here he creates for himself a sense of importance, holding his squalid court as father of the Marshalsea, accepting as his right the untiring devotion and willing service of Little Dorrit and receiving with condescension the little tips and gifts of cigars which he has managed to establish as the perquisites due to his self-imposed consequence. His sudden access of wealth leads to an extension of his delusions of grandeur into the wider field of expensive continental travel until he suddenly crumbles at a grand party, surprising the guests with an astonishing after dinner speech when he believes himself to be back in prison once more. It is a masterly study with a deep sadness running through it.

Repression pervades the whole book. Mrs. Clennam suffers from hysterical paralysis as the result of her deception and fraud, living her life in a wheelchair under self-imposed duress until the threat of discovery induces such a dramatic compulsion that she is released into a brief moment of wild activity before subsiding once more into paralysis and silence. Tattycoram tries hard to be constrained but is the one who always manages to break away, even in the end, from the curious relationship she has established with that self-tormented character Miss Wade. Mr. Merdle, despite his robust constitution, has an undiagnosed complaint of psychosomatic origin. The restrictions are not only physical and psychological but governmental as well. The Circumlocation Office imposes its dead hand on the life of England, blocking initiative, discouraging inventiveness and lowering incentive.

Plate 9   Coavinses (Skimpole).

Plate 10   The Family Portraits at Mrs. Bayham Badger's (Badger).

Plate 11　Sir Leister Dedlock (Skimpole).

Plate 12　The Patriotic Conference (Physician).

Sir Henry Thompson, 1820-1904.

Oil painting: a dinner given by Sir H. Thompson for Dr. Ernest Hart; by Solomon J. Solomon, not dated. In the Wellcome Inst. (no. 2507/1940). *Note:* subjects are (l. to r.) Sir R. Quain, Sir J. Paget, Sir V. Horsley, Sir H. Thompson, E. Hart, Sir A. Critchett, Sir T. S. Wells, Sir W. Broadbent, Sir J. Fayer, butler, Sir L. Brunton. *By courtesy of the Wellcome Trustees.*

Plate 13. Under the Plane Tree (Manette).

Plate 14. Vignette Title (Manette).

Plate 15   The Shoemaker (Manette).

Plate 16   Congratulations (Manette).

Plate 17. The Knock at the Door (Manette).

Plate 18. After the Sentence (Manette).

In *Little Dorrit* there is still less of that extravagant and hilarious characterisation which had brought Dickens to fame, a graver tone, a more studied artistry and a consistently impressive atmosphere have developed. Dickens has become more successful in depicting virtue and emotion without embarrassment than in *Bleak House*. Though *Little Dorrit* never acquires the force of that fierce tale, it is notable that Amy's unclouded goodness never really cloys. The two doctors mark the transition. Dr. Haggage is cast in the old Dickensian mould but is soon done with. Physician is developed in the new thoughtful manner without caricature and with a far greater depth of understanding than before. Though not dull like Allan Woodcourt, he has none of the sparkle of Sir Parker Peps or Sir Tumley Snuffim; he is interesting and serious, devoid of charlatanism or hypocrisy. Physician is a fascinating brief study of one of the great fictional doctors of literature.

Little Dorrit doesn't start with the birth of Amy. The story opens in a prison in Marseilles, moves on to Mrs. Clennam's dingy, old house, propped up with supports and destined to collapse, situated somewhere between Cheapside and the river, before going back to the birth of Little Dorrit in the Marshalsea prison. Dickens thus just avoided starting yet another of his novels with a doctor attending the birth of his principal character. However, when he does appear, this doctor is found to be a vintage specimen. Dr. Haggage, an old inmate of the prison, is summoned by the turnkey when Mrs. Dorrit goes into labour while she is visiting her husband confined for debt. Dr. Haggage is assisted by Mrs. Bangham, charwoman and messenger, the prison's popular medium of communication with the outer world. When the turnkey arrives to fetch the doctor he is playing all-fours (Ch. 6), smoking and drinking brandy with a friend.

> The doctor's friend was in the positive degree of hoarseness, puffiness, red-facedness, all-fours, tobacco, dirt and brandy; the doctor in the comparative — hoarser, puffier, more red-faced, more all-fourey, tobaccoer, dirtier and brandier. The doctor was amazingly shabby, in a torn and

darned rough-weather sea-jacket, out at elbows and
eminently short of buttons (he had been in his time the experienced surgeon carried by a passenger ship), the dirtiest
white trousers conceivable by mortal man, carpet slippers,
and no visible linen. "Childbed?" said the doctor. "I'm the
boy!"

The special feature of the treatment adopted by Dr. Haggage is
that he keeps Mrs. Bangham up to the mark with a little brandy
so that she can the better ward off the flies. He repeats this treatment every hour but, having administered her potion, takes care
to see that he gets his own. At last:

> "A very nice little girl indeed", said the doctor; "little but
> well-formed. Halloa Mrs. Bangham! You're looking queer!
> You be off, ma'am, this minute, and fetch a little more
> brandy, or we shall have you in hysterics".

To Mr. Dorrit's distress that his child should be born inside the
lock, the doctor offers this consolation:

> "Bah, bah, sir, what does it signify? A little more elbow-
> room is all we want here. We are quiet here; we don't get
> badgered here; there's no knocker here, sir, to be hammered
> at by creditors and bring a man's heart into his mouth.
> Nobody comes here to ask if a man's at home, and to say
> he'll stand on the door mat till he is. Nobody writes
> threatening letters about money to this place. It's freedom,
> sir, it's freedom!"

So Amy Dorrit is born, "her first draught of air" is "tinctured"
with Dr. Haggage's brandy and she has a turnkey for a godfather.
    The next brief medical interlude occurs when John Baptist
Cavalletto, one of the two prisoners the story starts with in
Marseilles, arrives in London and on his first evening is run over
by one of the Mails racing dangerously round St. Paul's at twelve
or fourteen miles an hour. He is befriended by Arthur Clennam,
who is passing (1, Ch.13), and taken to Saint Bartholomew's.

After trying the leg with a finger and two fingers, and one hand and two hands, and over and under, and up and down, and in this direction and in that, and approvingly remarking on the points of interest to another gentleman who joined him, the surgeon at last clapped the patient on the shoulder, and said, "He won't hurt. He'll do very well. It's difficult enough, but we shall not want him to part with his leg this time."

The surgeon then diagnoses:

"A compound fracture above the knee and a dislocation below. They are both of a beautiful kind." He gave the patient a friendly clap on the shoulder again, as if he really felt that he was a very good fellow indeed, and worthy of all commendation for having broken his leg in a manner interesting to science.

Doctor Buchan's Domestic Medicine is opened a number of times but more as an excuse than as a source of information. Mrs. Tickit, cook and housekeeper to the Meagles, is apt to sit peering over the parlour blind all day whenever the family goes away, looking for their return. She always had Dr. Buchan's book on her knee (1. Ch. 16) but in it she was said to have found no balsam for a wounded mind. This is hardly Dr. Buchan's fault:

the lucubrations of which learned practitioner, Mr. Meagles implicitly believed she had never yet consulted to the extent of one word in her life.

Mr. Merdle lives in Harley Street (1. Ch. 21), Cavendish Square.

Like unexceptionable Society, the opposing rows of houses in Harley Street were very grim with one another. Indeed, the mansions and their inhabitants were so much alike in that respect, that the people were often to be found drawn up on opposite sides of dinner-tables, in the shade of their own loftiness, staring at the other side of the way with the dulness of the houses.

Mr. Merdle is immensely rich and:

> Harley Street, Cavendish Square, was more than aware of
> Mr. and Mrs. Merdle. Intruders there were in Harley Street,
> of whom it was not aware; but Mr. and Mrs. Merdle it
> delighted to honour. Society was aware of Mr. and Mrs.
> Merdle.

Mr. Merdle provides the money, Mrs. Merdle the manner.

> This great and fortunate man had provided that extensive
> bosom, which required so much room to be unfeeling
> enough in, with a nest of crimson and gold some fifteen
> years before. It was not a bosom to repose upon, but it was a
> capital bosom to hang jewels upon. Mr. Merdle wanted
> something to hang jewels upon, and he bought it for the
> purpose.

Mr. Merdle's doctor knows everybody and everybody knows
him. At a party he comes up to Mr. Merdle and touches him on
the arm.

> Mr. Merdle started. "Oh! It's you!"
> "Any better today?"
> "No", said Mr. Merdle, "I am no better."
> "A pity I didn't see you this morning. Pray come to me
> tomorrow, or let me come to you."

Bar and Bishop, who are standing by, comment on this exchange
to Physician when Mr. Merdle has gone, before offering a
diagnosis, Bishop throwing in a recommended treatment for good
measure. Physician, however, can find nothing the matter with
Mr. Merdle, he says that he has:

> the constitution of a rhinoceros, the digestion of an ostrich,
> and the concentration of an oyster. As to nerves, Mr. Merdle
> is of cool temperament, and not a sensitive man: is about as
> invulnerable, I should say, as Achilles. How such a man
> should suppose himself unwell without reason, you may
> think strange. But I have found nothing the matter with

him. He may have some deep-seated recondite complaint. I can't say. I only say, that at present I have not found it out.

At the dinner party specially designed to bring Lord Decimus and Mr. Merdle together (2. Ch. 12), everyone is in a state of agitation.

> Bishop alone talked steadily and evenly. He conversed with the great Physician on that relaxation of the throat with which young curates were too frequently afflicted, and on the means of lessening the great prevalence of that disorder in the church. Physician, as a general rule, was of opinion that the best way to avoid it was to know how to read, before you made a profession of reading. Bishop said dubiously, did he really think so? And Physician said, decidedly, yes he did.
>
> Few ways of life (2. Ch. 25) were hidden from Physician, and he was oftener in its darkest places than even Bishop. There were brilliant ladies about London who perfectly doted on him, my dear, as the most charming creature and the most delightful person, who would have been shocked to find themselves so close to him if they could have known on what sights those thoughtful eyes of his had rested within an hour or two, and near to whose beds, and under what roofs, his composed figure had stood. But Physician was a composed man, who performed neither on his own trumpet, nor on the trumpets of other people. Many wonderful things did he see and hear, and much irreconcilable moral contradiction did he pass his life among; yet his equality of compassion was no more disturbed than the Divine Master's of all healing was. He went, like the rain, among the just and unjust, doing all the good he could, and neither proclaiming it in the synagogues nor on the corners of streets. . . . Where he was, something real was. And half a grain of reality, like the smallest portion of some other scarce natural productions, will favour an enormous quantity of diluent.
>
> It came to pass, therefore, that Physician's little dinners always presented people in their least conventional lights.

The guests said to themselves, whether they were conscious of it or no, "Here is a man who really has an acquaintance with us as we are, who is admitted to some of us every day with our wigs and paint off, who hears the wanderings of our minds, and sees the undisguised expression of our faces, when both are past our control; we may as well make an approach to reality with him, for the man has got the better of us and is too strong for us". Therefore, Physician's guest came out so surprisingly at his round table that they were almost natural.

Physician's round table dinners were probably inspired by the Octave dinners given by Sir Henry Thompson at which Dickens was at times one of the distinguished guests.

Physician did not find out Mr. Merdle's complaint until he found him, with his jugular vein severed, dead in a bath with an empty laudanum-bottle and a tortoise-shell handled penknife on the side:

the greatest Forger and the greatest Thief that ever cheated the gallows.

Interlude 1857 - 1860

Forster in his biography of Dickens (Forster, 2.458) wrote of "that sorrowful period of 1857 - 8, when, . . . a vaguely disturbed feeling for the time took possession of him, and occurrences led to his adoption of other persuits than those to which till then he had given himself exclusively". The term "vaguely disturbed" is a fine understatement to describe the emotional upheaval which Dickens was experiencing. The "occurrences" were a formal separation from his wife and a tumultuous love affair with a girl of 18, the "other persuits" were the dramatic public readings of his works on which he embarked at that time.

Much evidence has come to light in the last 40 years, and a great deal has been written about this affair such as the establishments which Dickens set up for the young actress Ellen Ternan, the entries of journeys in his diary in 1867, their involvement in the train accident at Staplehurst on their return from a visit to France and the effect that all this had on his life and work. Experts assert that there are no grounds for assuming as a fact that Ellen Ternan was ever his mistress and that there is quite a lot of evidence against it. It is most improbable that the exact nature of such a relationship will ever be established; Felix Aylmer reminded us that Mahomet demanded the sworn evidence of four eye-witnesses to the offence before he would allow the death penalty for adultery. Ellen Ternan knew Charles Dickens for thirteen years, she married, at the age of 37, six years after his death. He paid the rates on her home under an assumed name until his death, visited her frequently and travelled with her abroad. Such circumstances, in their day, must have imposed on them an almost intolerable strain. It seems to me that a purely spiritual relationship would have been unlikely, uncharacteristic and uncharitable the one to the other.

By 1855 Dickens was thoroughly unsettled. He found it particularly difficult to get started on *Little Dorrit*. His fame, though very gratifying, had led to too many distractions in public life while his private life was no longer satisfying. Things were getting on his nerves. His wife had not developed with his success; she had a placid, affectionate and rather lazy disposition and had been so occupied and confined with 10 children and 4 miscarriages in 15 years that this had allowed her more alert sister Georgina, who had lived with them since she was 15, to take her place not only in running her house and family but in being escorted to functions by her husband. At this point, out of the blue after 22 years, Dickens received a letter from Maria Beadnell (then Mrs. Winter) his first love and the model for Dora in *David Copperfield*. His response was immediate and romantic, just when he was convincing himself that he and Kate were totally unsuited to one another he was presented with a chance to meet his first love again in secret. He wrote to Maria to ask her to tell her daughter that he had "loved her mother with the most extraordinary earnestness". Romantically the meeting was a disaster, his dark little beauty Maria had become a tubby matron, but, as a vagary of human experience and caprice of fortune, the encounter was turned to good effect as she made a second appearance in *Little Dorrit* as Flora Finching, who was not only broad, short of breath, diffuse and silly, but, having been spoiled and artless years ago, was determined to be spoiled and artless still. His ready search for renewed romance had been thwarted.

In 1857, when *Little Dorrit* was finished, Dickens, in his restless state, found an outlet in acting. He was then living at Tavistock House, where the British Medical Association building now stands, and had erected there a theatre for his amateur theatricals. He acted with Wilkie Collins in a play of his on which they had worked together called *The Frozen Deep* and threw himself into it with great energy even growing a beard, designed to fit the part of Richard Wardour the arctic explorer, which was to become the hallmark of his public image. They decided to take the play to Manchester and engage actresses to take the parts which had been played by Dickens's daughters. Mrs. Ternan and her daughters Ellen and Maria were chosen and started rehearsals at Tavistock House. The cast also performed *Uncle John* in which Dickens played the part of an old gentleman who fell in love with a young girl. He, now 46 years old, fell violently in love with Ellen, a state of infatuation for which the past few years had so well prepared him. That autumn he ran away from it all ("I want to escape from myself, my misery is amazing") after a long hot summer, going on his *Lazy Tour* with Wilkie Collins to whom he wrote (Forster, 2.458) in March 1858: "I have never known a moment's peace or content, since the last night of *The Frozen Deep*. I do suppose that there never was a man so seized and rendered by one spirit."

Dickens had changed. He wanted to break with his old life. He destroyed letters he had received from all the people he had known and loved, throwing them in their unopened packets on a bonfire saying: "Would to God every letter I had ever written was on that pile!" He needed money since he now had to provide for his wife, look after his family aged 6, 8, 10, 12, 13, 17, 18, 19 and 20, keep his home, still run by his sister-in-law Georgina, improve Gad's Hill, the house of his youthful dreams which had become his at last, and set up an establishment for Ellen. His readings of his works for charity had been a great success and now, against Forster's advice, he decided to become a professional reader. This activity not only brought in a great deal of money but also provided a much needed and immediate emotional outlet through his considerable histrionic ability. Instant public acclaim and quick financial return were far more in tune with his mood as well as with his growing needs than the writer's accustomed discipline of solitary, prolonged creative work. *A Tale of Two Cities* was the one novel to come out of "that sorrowful period".

By the end of 1860, settled at last both at Gad's Hill and in the pattern of his new life, he started once more to write a novel in the great tradition, which, like *David Copperfield*, was to be told in the first person. This was *Great Expectations* of which George Gissing wrote: "In the general estimate of 'David Copperfield' Mr. Swinburne concurs; he is disposed to name with it as the novelist's second best book, 'Great Expectations', a judgement for which something may be said when it is considered how wonderfully Dickens returned, without repeating himself, in the shorter story, to the autobiography of his childhood, a subject which brought out his finest qualities". This time, however, on a graver, self-depreciatory note, with a hero who needed to be loved for what he was, not for what he did, and who had to submit to the humiliation of being forgiven. It is natural to wonder how much of Ellen may have gone into Estella.

There is a surgeon in *Great Expectations* who appears when Mrs. Joe Gargary is felled by a convict's leg-iron, and suffers an injury to the brain. There is also "our local practitioner" encountered at the "Three Jolly Bargemen" and another surgeon who attends to Miss Havisham's burns. No doctor takes a real part in the action, however, although the medical interest is as great in this as in any of Dickens's novels. One almost did so in the form of a Shropshire doctor originally intended to be Estella's second husband instead of Pip, but Bulwer Lytton intervened and persuaded the none too reluctant Dickens to write the alternative "happy ending" which is so out of key with what had gone before and denies Pip his final release.

The Lazy Tour of Two Idle Apprentices (1857)

(with Wilkie Collins)

In the autumn of 1857 two idle apprentices of a highly meritorious lady named Literature ran away from their employer after a long hot summer and the long hot work it had brought with it. One of them was running away from another highly disturbing lady as well. In their travels they reached Carlisle on market day "disagreeably and reproachfully busy" where there was one stall with a medical flavour. This (Ch. 1) was:

> "Doctor Mantle's Dispensary for the cure of all Human Maladies and no charge for advice", and with Doctor Mantle's "Laboratory of Medical, Chemical, and Botanical Science" — both healing institutions established on one pair of trestles, one board and one sun-blind.

Mr. Thomas Idle, unwisely and most unidly, decided to climb Carrock Fell, sprained his ankle and was in need of a real doctor. From the inn in the little town in Cumberland they sent Jock (Ch. 2) for Doctor Speddie.

> A tall, thin, large boned, old gentleman, with an appearance at first sight of being hard-featured; but, at a second glance, the mild expression of his face and some particular touches of sweetness and patience about his mouth, corrected this impression and assigned his long professional rides, by day and night, in the bleak hill-weather, as the true cause of that appearance.

77

His coat was darned and his linen frayed.

> He might have been poor—it was likely enough in that
> out-of-the-way spot—or he might have been a little self-
> forgetful and eccentric. Any one could have seen directly,
> that he had neither wife nor child at home. He had a
> scholarly air with him, and that kind of considerate humani-
> ty towards others which claimed a gentle consideration for
> himself.
> "Gently, Jock, gently", said the Doctor as he advanced
> with a quiet step. "Gentlemen a good evening. I am sorry
> that my presence is required her. A slight accident, I hope?
> A slip and a fall? Yes, yes, yes. Carrock, indeed? Hah! Does
> that pain you, sir? No doubt it does. It is the great connect-
> ing ligament here, you see, that has been badly strained.
> Time and rest, sir! They are often the recipe in greater
> cases", with a slight sigh, "and often the recipe in small. I
> can send a lotion to relieve you, but we must leave the cure
> to time and rest."

Thomas Idle's companion Francis Goodchild goes back with
the doctor to fetch the lotion but they fall into conversation and
the doctor's assistant, Mr. Lorn, is dispatched with the prescription while they sit and talk. This Mr. Lorn is remarkable: at least
52 years old, pale with large black eyes, sunken cheeks, iron-grey
hair and wasted hands. "There was no vestige of colour in the
man". Doctor Speddie tells Francis Goodchild one of those
macabre tales about him packed with coincidences of which
Dickens was so fond.

Arthur Holliday, a young man who took after his father in the
wildness of his youth, the son of a rich manufacturer, had arrived
in Doncaster many years before in the middle of race-week and
been unable to find a room for the night. At last after many trials
he was offered a bed in a small pub called "The Two Robins", if
he would share with another gentleman and pay in advance. He
was assured that the other man was a quiet well-behaved person
who had gone to bed already. He accepted only to find that his
room mate had died at 5 o'clock that afternoon. Unable to sleep

he tried to keep his candle alight, but eventually overcome with curiosity he decided to look at the face of the dead man, he lifted the sheet to find that his eyes were open and that he was moving. He aroused the house; the doctor sent for was Doctor Speddie who revived the corpse. The man turned out to be a medical student who believed that he owed his life to Arthur Holliday but appeared shocked on learning his name. Coincidences were then piled one upon another for it turned out that this Mr. Lorn was the illegitimate son of Arthur's father and was engaged to marry the girl Arthur was in love with. Mr. Lorn left early in the morning and never communicated with his fiancée again, she eventually married Arthur and died a few years later, telling Doctor Speddie her side of the story. Arthur married again. Years later Mr. Lorn applied for the post of Dr. Speddie's assistant; although they recognised each other at once, neither had ever referred to their first meeting when Mr. Lorn was brought back from the dead.

Reprinted, 1858

The Detective Police

Sergeant Dornton's story 'The Adventures of a Carpet Bag' contains a rather incidental but most villainous doctor. Sergeant Dornton is searching for a man who "had been carrying on, pretty heavily, in the bill-stealing way". All he knows about him is his name, that he is a Jew and that he has with him a carpet bag which has on one side of it, worked in worsted, a green parrot on a stand. Not a bad start. However, the man has escaped to the United States. Many months later Sergeant Dornton has a stroke of luck, being sent to America to apprehend a man who has robbed a bank in Ireland of several thousand pounds, the infamous Doctor Dunday who is supposed to have bought a farm in New Jersey. The sergeant traps him in New York, claps him into prison and hauls him before the magistrate. There, in the magistrate's room, is a carpet bag with a green parrot worked in worsted and there, in prison, is the Jewish bill-stealer in custody for another offence, and there, in the carpet bag is the evidence relating to the frauds for which the sergeant has been vainly endeavouring to take him. The sergeant not only gets his man but the evil Doctor Dunday for good measure.

Our Bore

Our bore is admitted on all hands to be a good-hearted man. He may put fifty people out of temper, but he keeps his own. He preserves a sickly solid smile upon his face, when other faces are ruffled by the perfection he has attained in his art, and has an equable voice which never travels out of one key or rises above one pitch. His manner is a manner of tranquil interest. None of his opinions are startling. Among his deepest-rooted convictions, it may be mentioned that he considers the air of England damp, and holds that our lively neighbours—he always calls the French our lively neighbours—have the advantage of us in that particular.

He is a bore on travel, on scenery, on pictures, on the East, on politics, on buildings, on London, on everything he mentions. At one period of his life he has unfortunately had an illness, and thereafter he drags his listeners through the whole of his symptoms, progress and treatment. He feels a tightness he can't account for:

> accompanied with a constant sensation as if he were being stabbed—or, rather, jobbed—that expresses it more correctly—jobbed—with a blunt knife.

He gets sparks before his eyes, waterwheels in his head and hammers down his back. He seeks advice.

> He naturally thought of Callow, at that time one of the most eminent physicians in London, and he went to Callow. Callow said, "Liver!" and prescribed rhubarb and calomel, low diet, and moderate exercise.

He loses confidence in Callow and goes to Moon, whom half the town was then mad about. Moon said "Kidneys!" . . . gave strong acids, cupped, and blistered. Clatter said "Accumulation of fat about the heart!" Snugglewood said "Brain!" They all applied leeches, and ministered enormous quantities of medicine and kept him low. But, then he saw Jilkins—at that period in a very small practice, with, however, a rising reputation among the people in the know. Jilkins said:

> "You have been humbugged. This is a case of indigestion, occasioned by deficiency of power in the stomach. Take a mutton chop in half-an-hour, with a glass of the finest old sherry that can be got for money. Take two mutton chops

to-morrow, and two glasses of the finest old sherry. Next day, I'll come again." In a week our bore was on his legs, and Jilkins's success dates from that period!

Jilkins knew his man, as well as the patter. An old physician once said to me "be definite", say "cabbage certainly, cauliflower on no account". Such a welcome prescription combined with a firm denigration of all that had gone before and associated with an acceptable diagnosis such as "deficiency of power in the stomach" was calculated to assure success if the patient was bored, wealthy, underemployed, neglected and gullible. There are not quite so many Jilkinses about as there used to be. Medical practice is becoming more difficult.

A Tale of Two Cities (1859)

This is the only Dickens novel in which the central character is a doctor despite the fact that Forster in his account of *A Tale of Two Cities* in the *Life* fails to mention Dr. Manette, who is seldom absent from the march of events, or that Una Pope-Hennessy, in her summary of the plot, gives Dr. Manette no more than incidental mention. Superficially *A Tale of Two Cities* may appear to be no more than a semi-historical, romantic tale with a background of the French Revolution. In it Darnay, a French emigré, revolts against his aristocratic origins and the cruel and high-handed behaviour of his family and marries Lucie Manette, the daughter of a doctor who has suffered long and shameful imprisonment in the Bastille at the command of his relations for their own protection. Darnay returns to France on a mission of mercy after the revolution has broken out, is arrested, sentenced to death and saved by Sydney Carton, a dissolute lawyer bearing a strong resemblance to him, who takes his place on the guillotine for love of Darnay's wife. As such it is not one of Dickens's greatest novels; it was written at a difficult time in his life chiefly to support his new weekly periodical *All The Year Round,* it has less dialogue than before, concentrating on incident rather than character. There is, however, a good deal more to it than this.

At one time Dickens thought of calling this book *The Doctor of Beauvais.* Dr. Manette is at the centre of the whole tale passing from a young successful practitioner of 27 years of age (whose story is not told until the end), to become a revengeful prisoner writing a searing condemnation of every member of the family which had secured his internment; to be turned into a solitary, depressed, psychological wreck—One Hundred and Five North Tower—who clings to scraps of sanity through continuous application to repetitive work; to be revived and rehabilitated as a man of 45 practising medicine once more, but still liable to relapse under stress, who returns to France a hero with "impetuous confidence" to be appointed the inspecting physician to three prisons; to become the saviour of his son-in-law only tragically to find that he is used as his final accuser; and so to his last relapse into a meandering old man, helpless and inarticulate though still no more than 60 years of age. It is his story which raises this novel to a true Dickensian level.

Darnay displays none of the style of his ancestors, runs his neck into every trap, is three times tried for his life and each time has to be rescued by others. Sydney Carton is not even realistically dissolute and can only be forgiven the infliction of those maudlin confessions on Lucie Manette because of his magnificent and famous end. Lucie is all dove-like devotion and, although it grates, the dreadful, almost unforgiveable, farewell of her dying child can hardly be blamed on her. The minor characters like Cruncher and Miss Pross only come sporadically to life in most uncharacteristic fashion. Mr. Stryver is a real person and Mr. Lorry sensible, staunch and true but it is the Marquis and particularly the Defarges who do most to enrich the story. The Doctor's theme "recalled to life" pervades the book: resurrectionists abound from Cruncher who opens coffins, Cly who comes back to life never having got into his, and Miss Pross's brother Solomon who appears at last as Barsad the spy. Dr. Manette stays at the imaginative heart of it all.

This is a most intriguing account of the effect of prolonged solitary confinement and of the permanent psychological damage it may do. When Dickens visited the Eastern Penitentiary in Philadelphia he wrote with horror in *American Notes* (Ch. 7) of what he had seen and asserted that no man had a right to inflict solitary confinement on his fellow-creatures.

> I hold this slow and daily tampering with the mysteries of the brain, to be immeasurably worse than any torture of the body: and because its ghastly signs and tokens are not so palpable to the eye and sense of touch as scars upon the

flesh; because its wounds are not upon the surface, and it extorts few cries that human ears can hear; therefore I the more denounce it, as a secret punishment which slumbering humanity is not roused up to stay.

Such words deserve attention today when the idea is abroad once more that scars upon the mind are of little consequence so long as there are no scars upon the flesh for all to see. Slumbering humanity has to be roused up to stay this returning evil. The psychiatrists should have been the first, the loudest and the most persistent in crying "we the more denounce it". Too often, their tardy, weak and guarded disapproval of mental torture, whether for political ends or as an anti-terrorist measure and irrespective of whether it has been used in this country or in any other, has been shameful. Those who have unhesitatingly spoken out in firm condemnation have raised our spirits. Doctors should read Dickens for the anger, still so relevant to our needs, as well as for the entertainment which gives such balm to the spirit.

Christmas Stories (1867)

Mrs. Lirriper's Legacy

I have a great weakness for Mrs. Lirriper, Major Jackman, Miss Wozenham, Jemmy, The United Grand Junction Lirriper and Jackman Great Norfolk Palour Line, and all the inhabitants of Norfolk Street, Strand. The Major's manner of dealing with Mr. Buffle the tax collector is joyous and masterly, he rescues the Buffles from the great fire and unites Miss Buffle with her articled young gentleman while Mrs. Lirriper is saving her rival boarding house keeper Miss Wozenham.

The late Mr. Lirriper has a younger brother, a doctor, described by Mrs. Lirriper (Ch. 1) in her own special and most delectable style:

> Doctor of what I am sure it would be hard to say unless Liquor, for neither Physic nor Music nor yet Law does Joshua Lirriper know a morsel of except continually being summoned to the County Court and having orders made upon him which he runs away from, and once was taken in the passage of this very house with an umbrella up and the Major's hat on, giving his name with the door-mat round him as Sr. Johnson Jones, K.C.B. in spectacles residing at the Horse Guards.

Joshua is a bad lot, he is in debt and a grand cadger. Before his brother's funeral he wrote:

> "One single sovereign would enable me to wear a decent suit of mourning for my much-loved brother. I vowed at the time of his lamented death that I would ever wear sables in

memory of him but Alas how short-sighted is man, How keep that vow when penniless!"

No Thoroughfare (with Wilkie Collins)

Dickens was much given to improbabilities, a weakness which seemed to come to a head when collaborating with Wilkie Collins. In this tale they pushed their coincidental contrivances to the limit. The doctor in *No Thoroughfare* merely comes in at the end to provide the third piece of evidence which clinches the identity of Mrs. Jane Miller's adopted son. Doctor Ganz of Neuchâtel is no more than a signature on a certificate. Improbabilities and the frequency of the unexpected are so interesting in real life: the careful research into upsets of the laws of chance, the uncertainty principle at the very heart of physics, and the difficulty of distinguishing significant from trivial coincidences are all so intriguing that it is easy to become impatient with the contrived literary manufacture of coincidence merely to enhance a plot or to save effort. Generally speaking they should be used in fiction with great discretion. Discretion was not one of Dickens's outstanding characteristics but, with genius, who cares.

The incredible plot of *No Thoroughfare* starts outside the Foundling Hospital where a veiled lady persuades a young nurse, against the rules, to divulge the name that has been given to her child admitted to the hospital that day. Twelve years later she comes back to adopt a child, choosing the one named Walter Wilding, the name she had been given as being that of her own son. Thirteen years later, having told him that she is his mother, she dies leaving him the business of Wilding & Co., Wine Merchants which he runs with his partner George Vendale. Walter Wilding engages a housekeeper who turns out to be the young nurse we started with, now widowed. It had been the practice in the Foundling to use names over again when children left to be adopted, and the housekeeper now reveals that the first Walter Wilding, the veiled lady's child, had been adopted and taken to Switzerland before she came back to seek her son. Walter Wilding the second, dies after vainly searching for the rightful heir to the business, while his partner, working with him all along (nearly murdered in the mountains by a thief and swindler who is his fiancée's guardian) turns out to be the first Walter Wilding, the very boy who came back from Switzerland to Groombridge-Wells with his adopted parent Mrs. Jane Miller. Identity established by Dr. Ganz, he inherits a fortune and marries his love.

This rather depressing sequence of improbabilities contains what is perhaps Dickens's most often quoted reference to a doctor's prescription. Madame Dor, George Vendale's fiancée's companion (Act. 1), is sitting in church and:

> turning her back upon everybody and everything, could not fail to be Ritualistically right at some moment of the service; like the man whom the doctors recommended to get drunk once a month, and who, that he might not overlook it, got drunk every day.

Conclusion

Dickens was only 58 when he died in June 1870 from a cerebral haemorrhage. From an early age he had had attacks of violent spasm in his left side. He suffered excruciating pain associated with fever while working in the warehouse and Bob Fagin filled empty blacking-bottles with hot water and applied them to his side. The pain was severe, unilateral, and appears to have been typical of renal colic (which strictly speaking is neither renal nor colic) due to stones in the upper urinary tract. When he was 32 years old, running home in Genoa one night because the gates were closed at midnight he crashed into a pole stretched across the street, fell heavily and had a return of agonising pain in his side. He is likely to have suffered some kidney damage associated with these repeated attacks of pain and fever which may have contributed to his arteriosclerosis of later life. In February 1865 while writing *Our Mutual Friend* he had had an attack of pain with lameness in his left foot which was to worry him for the rest of his life and which at that time "baffled experienced physicians". The boat train disaster at Staplehurst in June 1865 shook him badly, 10 were killed and many injured, though not himself harmed in body, the effect of the crash remained with him due to the horror, as he wrote to his doctor the next day, of working some hours among the dying and the dead. He did, however, retrieve the manuscript of *Our Mutual Friend* from the wreckage and wrote that Mr. and Mrs. Boffin had been in the accident and were much soiled but otherwise unhurt.

Dr. Francis Carr Beard (the brother of Thomas, his oldest friend, journalist, reporter with him in the House of Commons, best man at his wedding and godfather to his first born) had become Dickens's family doctor in 1859. He practised from 44

Welbeck St. Dickens wrote (Dexter, 1932) to him in 1861 "I should like to be inspected — though I hope I can offer no new attractions", and in 1866 sending tickets for one of his readings which was to include *Doctor Marigold:* "I hope you will like your brother-doctor".

Early in 1866 when *Our Mutual Friend* was finished he started on another tour of public readings. He soon became exhausted and developed pain in the left eye, hand and foot. Frank Beard (Forster, 2.250) said "Want of muscle power in the heart", Doctor Brinton of Brook Street said "Only remarkable irritability of the heart", both rather reminiscent of Clatter — Dickens only needed Callow, Snugglewood and Jilkins to collect a whole set of useless diagnoses. Matthew Arnold had just written:

> Nor bring to watch me cease to live
> Some Doctor, full of phrase and fame
> To shake his sapient head and give
> The ill he can not cure — a name.

In January 1867 Dickens was off again reading in Scotland and Ireland with a return of such pain in his left foot that, for a time, he could hardly walk. Sir Henry Thompson (Forster, 2.259) said "Bunion affected by the action of the shoe with erysipelas intervening". Twice in September he was seized in a most distressing manner apparently in the heart and began to have difficulty in sleeping. By November, despite it all, he went off again on a six months' reading tour in America. He had thought to get Ellen to join him but decided against it on arrival. He was soon laid on a bed in a state of collapse after a reading, and he contracted a severe catarrh which persisted throughout his American tour. He saw Dr. Fordyce Barker who wanted to stop the readings for a few days but Dickens refused. Landlord prescribed (Forster, 2.332) a "Rocky Mountain Sneezer" composed of brandy, rum and snow but even this had no effect. Dickens wrote (Forster, 2.333) that he had tried "Allopathy, homeopathy, cold things, warm things, sweet things, bitter things, stimulants, narcotics, all with the same effect. Nothing will touch it." The curious thing about his catarrh was that although it was distressing and persistent it was always good enough to leave him for the needful two hours of his performance.

His sleeplessness returned and he became exhausted by his readings, sustaining himself with an egg in sherry before he went on and taking another in the interval. Again he was forced to lie on a couch to recover after each performance. In Baltimore his catarrh was worse and he lost his voice, but, when it came to his reading, for that two hours, he was not even hoarse. Every night he came up to the mark "with spirits and spirit".

At the end of the tour he attended a public dinner in New York, spoke in pain and had to leave before the proceedings were over. Cerebro-vascular disease, a high state of excitement and considerable strain were all acting together to produce symptoms, with his physical and mental exhaustion being added to by lack of sleep induced by his over-active brain. Through it all he drove himself with an astonishing determination compounded of the exigence of his need for self expression, his power to move audiences, his response to instant acclaim and his persistent concern that he had a pressing necessity to make money. He earned £1300 a week in America (at 7 dollars to the pound!) and by the end of that tour had earned £33,000 in two years from his readings alone.

In May 1868 he sailed for home. The rest, the sea voyage and relief from the strain of his performances, did so much good that (Forster, 2.355) "My doctor was quite broken down in spirits on seeing me for the first time last Saturday. *Good lord! seven years younger!* said the doctor recoiling". Nevertheless, that summer he noticed that he could only read the halves of letters over shop doors when he looked to the right.

In October he set out on his last reading tour introducing a new performance, the murder in *Oliver Twist,* the most physically and emotionally exhausting he had yet attempted, a plan opposed once more by Forster. Again he fell ill with sickness and sleepless nights, his foot became worse and he saw Sir Henry Thompson once more who said "Gout!" and, with Frank Beard, signed a certificate to say that he was unfit to read. Rightly being sceptical of Sir Henry's diagnosis, Dickens then consulted Mr. James Syme (Forster, 2.360): "What made Thompson think it was gout? he said often, and seemed to take that opinion extremely ill". However, things didn't go much better when Syme said "An affection of the delicate nerves and muscles originating in cold . . . . Gout? Bah!"

Sir Henry Thompson was a most versatile man: surgeon, artist, connoisseur, writer and social reformer. His portrait by Sir John Millais is in the National Gallery, he is also to be seen in a group portrait in the Wellcome Museum and a self portrait entitled "Dining at the Palace" (alone, in attendance), is in the Royal College of Surgeons. A bust of him may also be seen at Golders Green for he was the founder of the Cremation Society. The group portrait is a painting of the guests at one of his Octave dinners, to which he invited eight people and served eight courses. These were regular events attended by many famous men such as the Prince of Wales, Herbert Asquith, Robert Browning, William Thackeray, John Leech, Rider Haggard, Conan Doyle and Charles Dickens. He was an expert on Nankin porcelain, wrote a novel called *Charley Kingston's Aunt* (the Aunt arriving as a corpse for dissection by Charley, a student in a Medical School). He operated on King Leopold of the Belgians and Napoleon III. His fees, worth something in those days, for these operations, performed for bladder stones, were £3000 and £2000 with £1000 for a second visit to Brussels for examination. His path had crossed that of Dickens once before when they had both been witnesses of the hanging of Mr. and Mrs. Manning in 1849 — Henry Thompson as a medical student and Dickens as a reporter writing an account for *The Times*.

James Syme, a controversial figure, Professor of Surgery in Edinburgh, was referred to as a "man of war" because he was always willing to battle for his principles. When Dean, he conducted a famous campaign against a Dr. Henderson for carrying on a homeopathic practice in the hospital. He was the father-in-law of Joseph Lister who wrote a fine tribute to him. Dr. John Brown, who was an apprentice of Syme's, added an essay on him to the re-issue of his *Horae Subsectivae. Locke and*

Sydenham and Other Papers, first published in 1866. He wrote: "He was I believe the greatest surgeon Scotland ever produced; and I cannot conceive of a greater, hardly as great a clinical teacher. . . . Sensitive, strong-willed, shy, having a stammer, bent upon reaching reality and the best of everything; he had to struggle with imperfect means, family disaster, and inadequate power of expressing his mind. He was full of genuine virtue and affection. . . . He was irritable at, and impatient of stupidity, and long-windedness and pretence; and at falsehood, quackery, and trickery of all sorts, he went like a terrier at a rat."

Nothing, and certainly no doctor, could stop Dickens for long, he was soon back reading again and "did" four Murders in one week. In April he wrote (Forster, 2.361): "My weakness and deadness are all on the left side; and if I don't look at anything I try to touch with my left hand, I don't know where it is". Frank Beard stopped the readings once more, warning that if he went on he could not guarantee that he would not go through life dragging a foot after him, and brought him back to see Sir Thomas Watson, finding, at last, a doctor to agree that he had been on the brink of an attack of paralysis on his left side, at risk of apoplexy, and that his symptoms were brought on by extreme hurry, overwork, and excitement incidental on his readings and that these could not be resumed with safety to himself. Dickens still insisted on giving twelve last readings, part of the remainder for which he had contracted. These he did early in 1870 with Frank Beard in attendance. Beard recorded his pulse rate in January 1870 as rising from 72 to 95 after reading from *David Copperfield* and the trial from *Pickwick Papers,* returning to normal in 15 minutes but in March 1870 his pulse rate was 120 after the murder of Nancy in *Oliver Twist* and, 7 days later, 35 minutes after a performance it still was running at 94. A record of his blood pressure would have been of interest. Again he could only read half of the shop signs on looking to the right and had a tendency to lose or misuse a word and to forget names and numbers. He also suffered, as he had done a few times before, a sudden rush of "internal haemorrhage", almost certainly from his haemorrhoids.

Sir Thomas Watson was president of the Royal College of Physicians from 1862 to 1867 and one of the most outstanding physicians of his day. His book entitled *Lectures on the Principles and Practice of Medicine* was the chief English textbook of medicine for more than thirty years. So lucid and scholarly were his writings that he was called "The Cicero of English Medicine".

Dickens had started to write his last book, *The Mystery of Edwin Drood*, in October 1869 between readings, and the first number appeared after his last reading in March 1870. Perhaps he was getting tired of doctors for when Mr. Crisparkle suggests to Jasper (looking ill on his return from a secret visit to the opium den) that the coming visit of his young nephew Edwin will do him more good than a doctor, Jasper replies: "More good than a dozen doctors. For I love him dearly, and I don't love doctors, or doctors' stuff." Dickens died on June 9th after writing in the chalet at Gad's Hill all day. His readings had surely helped to kill him and deprived the world of the end of his last fascinating book. W. H. Bowen set out to review Dickens's medical history, but expanded his account into a series of essays dealing with his principal family characters in a book published in 1956 called *Charles Dickens and his Family*. This contains much of interest but is far from being an impartial study. In dealing with his medical history it minimises the effect of the strain of his readings on his health and dismisses them as a factor contributing to his death. Bowen curiously considers that travelling by train, particularly fast ones, was more deleterious than the readings and (as with his treatment of Ellen) softens criticism, throws doubt on misbehaviour and even on wilful acts against the advice of his doctors. He insists that the trouble with Dickens's left foot during the last five years of his life was due to gout. This account, so full of assumptions and conjecture fails to meet Bowen's own strictures on previous references to Dickens's medical history which he described as "inaccurate because both superficial and speculative".

Dickens's break with his wife, his affair with Ellen Ternan and his public performances had changed his life. Ellen seems also to have influenced his ideas about women, there is a distinct change in the style of his last three heroines: Estella, Bella Wilfer and

Rose Bud. They seem to me to be a great improvement on many of those who had gone before with such a devoted show of angelic resignation. Estella is something quite new with her criminal parents, cold heart, expensive upbringing, haughty manner and outstanding beauty. Bella, always a favourite of mine, keeps trying to persuade herself that she is a mercenary and selfish wretch despite her good heart and kindly thoughtfulness for her endearing, innocent and chubby Pa. Lizzie Hexam, a secondary heroine, although once more all unselfish devotion, has a far tougher quality than the dear good heroines of the past. Rose "wonderfully pretty, wonderfully childish, wonderfully whimsical" nevertheless manages her Eddy with skill, generosity, compassion and humour. She keeps her good sense through an imposed engagement, the curiosity of Miss Twinketon's establishment, the jealousy of Neville Landless and her dreadful encounter with Jasper. This sensible, delicate but determined young woman is a most likeable character destined, we hope, to marry Lieutenant Tartar.

The Mystery of Edwin Drood showed Dickens at the end of his life not only writing with his old skill but outdoing his friend Wilkie Collins in the construction of a mystery story. Surely Forster learned the rights of this unfinished tale, however much people may delight in compounding the mystery. The gold ring was clearly planted on the body for the purpose of identification, Jasper has to be condemned, Crisparkle is certain to get Helen Landless and Mr. Grewgious is destined to triumph with the help of Datchery who must surely be his literary clerk Bazzard in disguise.

After Dickens's death some slips of writing were found within the leaves of another manuscript. They were the draft of a scene for *The Mystery of Edwin Drood* in which Sapsea, the "Old Tory jackass" of an auctioneer, speaks as he walks out of the Eight Club leaving them to make the best they can of becoming the Seven. This last fragment of Dickens's writing (Forster, 2.372) also contains his last doctor.

Another member of the Eight Club was Peartree; also

member of the Royal College of Surgeons. Mr. Peartree is
not accountable to me for his opinions, and I say no more of
them here than that he attends the poor gratis whenever
they want him, and is not the parish doctor. Mr. Peartree
may justify it to the grasp of *his* mind thus to do his
republican utmost to bring an appointed officer into contempt. Suffice it that Mr. Peartree can never justify it to the
grasp of *mine*.

Dickens's Doctors and Medical Students

1. *Sketches by Boz,* 1836
   Four Sisters
   Mr. Dawson   Surgeon attending Mrs. Robinson's confinement.

   Boarding House
   Dr. Wosky   Mrs. Bloss's physician.
   Septimus Hicks   Medical student.

2. *The Mudfog and Other Sketches,* 1837
   First meeting:
      Mr. Knight Bell
      Dr. W. R. Fee
      Dr. Kutankumagen
      Professor Muff
      Dr. Neeshawts
      Professor Nogo
      Dr. Toorell
   Second meeting:
      Dr. Grummidge
      Mortair
      Pessell
      Mr. Pipkin
      Dr. Soemup

3. *Pickwick Papers,* 1837
   Benjamin Allen   Medical student and doctor friend of Bob Sawyer.

   Gunter   Medical student.

Jack Hopkins	Medical student.
Nockemorf	Bob Sawyer's predecessor in practice in Bristol.
Noddy	Medical student.
Dr. Payne	Military surgeon of the 43rd.
Bob Sawyer	Medical student and doctor in Bristol and Bengal.
Dr. Slammer	Military surgeon of the 97th.
Slasher	Eminent surgeon at Saint Bartholomew's Hospital.

4; *Oliver Twist,* 1838

Mr. Losberne	Doctor to Mrs. Maylie and Rose Fleming.

5. *Nicholas Nickleby,* 1839

Dr. Lumbey	Doctor attending Mrs. Kenwig's confinement.
Sir Tumley Snuffim	Mrs. Wititterly's doctor.

6. *Martin Chuzzlewit,* 1844

Bevan	He seldom or never practised.
Dr. Ginery Dunkle	Spokesman at the Pogram levee, not certainly medical.
Dr. John Jobling	Anthony Chuzzlewit's doctor.
Lewsome	Medical assistant supplying poison to Jonas Chuzzlewit.

7. *Dombey & Son,* 1848

Sir Parker Peps	Court Physician present at Paul Dombey's birth and death.
Pilkins	Mr. Dombey's family doctor.

8. *The Battle of Life,* 1846 (Christmas Books, 1852)

Alfred Heathfield	Ward of the philosopher Dr. Anthony Jeddler.

9. *David Copperfield,* 1850

Mr. Chillip	Doctor attending Mrs. Copperfield at David's birth.

Plate 19. Eugene's Bedside (medical attendant).

Dr. William Brinton, 1823-1867.
By permission of the Royal College of Physicians of London.

Mr. James Syme, 1799-1870.
By permission of the Royal College of Surgeons of Edinburgh.

Sir Thomas Watson, 1792-1882.
By permission of the Royal College of Physicians of London.

10. *Bleak House,* 1853

Bayham Badger	Doctor in Chelsea, Mrs. Badger's third.
Allan Woodcourt	Marries Esther Summerson.
Harold Skimpole	Protégé of John Jarndyce.

11. *Little Dorrit,* 1857

Dr. Haggage	Marshalsea prisoner attending the birth of Amy Dorrit.
Physician	Doctor to Mr. Merdle, an experienced and wise practitioner.

12. *The Lazy Tour of Two Idle Apprentices,* 1857 (with Wilkie Collins)

Dr. Lorn	Assistant to Speddie.
Dr. Speddie	Treats Thomas Idle's sprained ankle.

13. *Reprinted,* 1858

Our Bore

Callow
Clatter
Jilkins   } A set of doctors making diagnoses and giving prescriptions.
Snugglewood

Detective Police

Dr. Dundey	Robbed a bank, apprehended in America, not certainly medical.

14. *A Tale of Two Cities,* 1859

Alexander Manette	Lucie's father, 18 years in the Bastille.

15. *Christmas Stories,* 1867

No Thoroughfare (with Wilkie Collins)

Dr. Ganz	Physician in Neuchâtel.

Mrs. Lirriper's Legacy

Dr. Joshua Lirriper	Younger brother of Mrs. Lirriper's late husband.

16.   *The Mystery of Edwin Drood,* 1870
      (a fragment found in manuscript)
      Peartree   M.R.C.S. and Member of the
                               Eight Club.

Bibliography

Aitken, Sir William, *The Science and Practice of Medicine,* Griffin, London, 1864.

Aylmer, F., *Dickens Incognito,* Rupert Hart-David, 1959.

Bathel, R., *The Longer I Live the More I Doubt the Doctors,* St. Mary's Hospital Gazette, 1970.

Bowen, W. H., *Charles Dickens and His Family,* W. Heffer and Sons, Cambridge, 1956.

Brain, Russell, 1st Baron Brain of Eynsham, *Dickensian Diagnoses,* The Purvis Oration delivered on the centenary of the West Kent Medico-Chirurgical Society, in *Some Reflections on Genius,* Pitman Medical Publishing Co. Ltd., London, 1960.

Brown, J., *Horae Subsectivae. Locke and Sydenham and Other Papers,* David Douglas, 6th Ed., Edinburgh, 1890.

Chesterton, G. K., *Charles Dickens,* Methuen & Co., 1906.

Conolly, John, *The Treatment of the Insane without Mechanical Restraints,* Smith, Elder, London, 1856.

Critchley, Macdonald, The Miss Havisham Syndrome, *History of Medicine,* 1969, 1, 2.

Cruikshank, G., *The Comic Almanack,* 1st Series, 1835 - 1843, Chatto & Windus.

Currie, T. R., A Few of Dickens's Doctors and Things Medical, *Pennsilvania Medical Journal,* 1908, 12, 134.

Da Costa, J. C., *Dickens's Doctors,* Philobiblon Club, Philadelphia, May 28, 1903.

Darwin, Bernard, Dickens's Doctors, The David Lloyd Roberts Memorial Lecture given at the Royal Society of Medicine, Oct. 1952. Reported in *British Medical Journal,* 1952, 2, 1039.

Dexter, W., *Dickens to His Oldest Friend* (including letters to Beard), Putnam, London, 1932.

Dickens and Medicine, Catalogue of the Centenary Exhibition of Books, Manuscripts and Prints at The Wellcome Institute of the History of Medicine, 1970.

Dickens, Dr. Charles, Physicians and Patients in Dickensian Works, *M.D.* Med. Newsmag., 1960, 4, 147.

Doggart, J., Dickens and the Doctors, *The Practitioner,* 1970, 204, 449.

Easton, E. R., Doctors in Dickens, *The Dickensian,* 1945, 41, 150.

Forster, J., *The Life of Charles Dickens,* 1872-4.

Green, F., *As Dickens Saw Them,* The Medical Profession, p. 62, Arthur H. Stockwell, 1933.

Green, R. M., Dickens's Doctors, *Boston Medical and Surgical Journal,* 1912, 166, 926.

Gissing's Writings on Dickens, Pierre Coastillas, Enitharmon Press, 1969.

Irvine, K., Dickensian Doctors, *Pulse,* Jan. 24, 1970.

Johnson, E., *Charles Dickens. His Tragedy and Triumph,* Little, Brown & Company, Boston, 1952.

Layton, T. B., Dickens's Medical Students, *Guy's Hospital Gazette,* 1936, 50, 553.

Leffmann, H., Dickens's Doctors, *The Dickensian,* 1907, 3, 268.

Lytton, E. B., 1st Baron Lytton, *Confession of a Water Patient,* H. Ballière, London, 1847.

Maidlow, W. H., A Note on Charles Dickens and The Doctors, *St. Bartholomew's Hospital Journal,* 1917, 24, 52.

Neely, R. D., *Doctors, Nurses and Dickens,* The Christopher Publishing House, Boston, 1939.

O'Day, K., Captain Jocy on Artificial Respiration, *British Medical Journal,* 1961, 1, 1543.

Pomeranz, H., Dickens's Doctors, *Medical Life,* 1935, 46, 56.

Pope-Hennessy, U., *Charles Dickens,* Chatto & Windus, 1945.

Schotte, L., Les Médecins dans l'oeuvre de Charles Dickens, *La Chronique Médicale,* 1909, 16, 657 and 689.

Shore, T. H. G., The Doctors of Dickens, *St. Bartholomew's Hospital Journal*, 1922, 29, 109.

Sprigge, S. S., The Medicine of Dickens, *Physic and Fiction,* Chapter IV, Hodder & Stoughton, 1921.

Strachan, C. G., The Medical Knowledge of Charles Dickens. Mrs. Gargary's Illness, *British Medical Journal*, 1924, 2, 780.

Ward, S. L., Medical Practice in the Days of Charles Dickens, Read before the Vancouver Fellowship, Oct. 1962, *British Columbia Med. J.*, 1963, 5, 521.

Index